Dinah Zike's
United States Government Reading and Study Skills

Glencoe

New York, New York   Columbus, Ohio   Chicago, Illinois   Peoria, Illinois   Woodland Hills, California

Glencoe

The *McGraw·Hill* Companies

Send all inquiries to:
Glencoe/McGraw-Hill
8787 Orion Place
Columbus, OH 43240-4027

ISBN 0-07-865917-5

Printed in the United States of America

3 4 5 6 7 8 9 10   045   08 07

Table of Contents

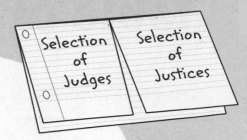

Chapter-Specific Foldables 43

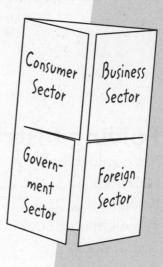

Dear Teacher,

What is a Foldable?

A Foldable is a 3-D, student-made, interactive graphic organizer based upon a skill. Making a Foldable gives students a fast, kinesthetic activity that helps them organize and retain information. Foldables can also be used for a more in-depth investigation of a concept, idea, opinion, event, or a person or place studied in a unit. The purpose of this ancillary is to show you how to create various types of Foldables and provide chapter-specific Foldables examples. With this information, you can individualize Foldables to meet your curriculum needs.

This book is divided into two sections. The first section presents step-by-step instructions, illustrations, and photographs of 34 Foldables. I've included over 100 photographs to help you visualize ways in which they might enhance instruction. The second section presents additional Foldables activities for each chapter in the textbook. I highly suggest making this book available as a source for students who wish to learn new and creative ways in which to make study guides, present projects, or do extra credit work.

Who Am I?

You may have seen Foldables featured in this book used in supplemental programs or staff-development workshops. Today my Foldables are used internationally. I present workshops and keynote addresses to over fifty thousand teachers and parents a year, sharing Foldables that I began inventing, designing, and adapting over thirty five years ago. Students of all ages are using them for daily work, note-taking activities, student-directed projects, forms of alternative assessment, journals, graphs, tables, and more.

Have fun using and adapting Foldables,

Dinah Zike

Why use Foldables in Social Studies?

When teachers ask me why they should take time to use the Foldables featured in this book, I explain that they:

- quickly organize, display, and arrange data, making it easier for students to grasp social studies concepts, theories, facts, opinions, questions, research, and ideas. They also help sequence events as outlined in the content standards.

- result in student-made study guides that are compiled as students listen for main ideas, read for main ideas, or conduct research.

- provide a multitude of creative formats in which students can present projects, research, interviews, and inquiry-based reports instead of typical poster board or social studies fair formats.

- replace teacher-generated writing or photocopied sheets with student-generated print.

- incorporate the use of such skills as comparing and contrasting, recognizing cause and effect, and finding similarities and differences into daily work and long-term projects. For example, these Foldables can be used to compare and contrast student explanations and/or opinions to explanations and/or opinions currently accepted by experts in the field of social studies.

- continue to "immerse" students in previously learned vocabulary, concepts, information, generalizations, ideas, and theories, providing them with a strong foundation that they can build upon with new observations, concepts, and knowledge.

- can be used by students or teachers to easily communicate data through graphs, tables, charts, models, and diagrams, including Venn diagrams.

- allow students to make their own journals for recording observations, research information, primary and secondary source data, surveys, and more.

- can be used as alternative assessment tools by teachers to evaluate student progress or by students to evaluate their own progress.

- integrate language arts, the sciences, and mathematics into the study of social studies.

- provide a sense of student ownership in the social studies curriculum.

Foldable Basics

What to Write and Where

Teach students to write general information such as titles, vocabulary words, concepts, questions, main ideas, and dates, on the front tabs of their Foldables. General information is viewed every time a student looks at a Foldable. Foldables help students focus on and remember key points without being distracted by other print.

Ask students to write specific information—supporting ideas, student thoughts, answers to questions, research information, empirical data, class notes, observations, and definitions—under the tabs.

As you teach, demonstrate different ways in which Foldables can be used. Soon you will find that students make their own Foldables and use them independently for study guides and projects.

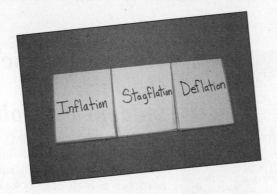

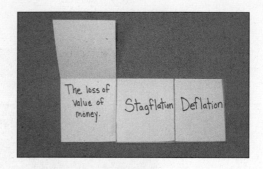

With or Without Tabs

Foldables with flaps or tabs create study guides that students can use to check what they know about the general information on the front of tabs. Use Foldables without tabs for assessment purposes or projects where information is presented for others to view quickly.

Venn Diagram used as a study guide

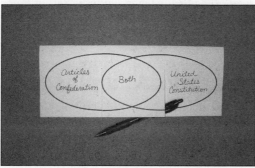

Venn Diagram used for assessment

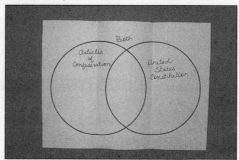

What to Do with Scissors and Glue

If it is difficult for your students to keep glue and scissors at their desks, set up a small table in the classroom and provide several containers of glue, numerous pairs of scissors (sometimes tied to the table), containers of crayons and colored pencils, a stapler, clear tape, and anything else you think students might need to make their Foldables. Don't be surprised if students donate colored markers, decorative-edged scissors, gel pens, stencils, and other art items to your publishing table.

The more they make and use graphic organizers, the faster students become at producing them.

Storing Graphic Organizers in Student Portfolios

Turn one-gallon freezer bags into student portfolios which can be collected and stored in the classroom. Students can also carry their portfolios in their notebooks if they place strips of two-inch clear tape along one side and punch three holes through the taped edge.

Have each student write his or her name along the top of the plastic portfolio with a permanent marker and cover the writing with two-inch clear tape to keep it from wearing off.

Cut the bottom corners off the bag so it won't hold air and will stack and store easily.

HINT: *I found it more convenient to keep student portfolios in my classroom so student work was always available when needed and not "left at home" or "in the car." Giant laundry-soap boxes make good storage containers for portfolios.*

Let Students Use This Book As an Idea Reference

Make this book of lists available to students to use as an idea reference for projects, discussions, social studies debates, extra credit work, cooperative learning group presentations, and more.

Using Visuals and Graphics with Foldables

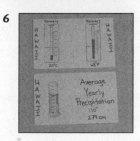

I designed the graphics on pages 8–11 to be used as visual aids for student production, while immersing students in measurement, percentages, maps, and time lines. At times, I require these graphics to be used in student presentations. I photocopy them or print them from my computer and pass them out. At other times, students incorporate them into their journals, notes, projects, and study guides independently. I found that students and teachers were more likely to use graphics if they were available on a classroom computer where they could be selected and printed out as needed.

1. Mark and label large United States and world maps to show where past and recent events occurred, where a historic person lived and worked, where wars were fought and battles won, where volcanoes are active and inactive, where boundaries of territories or regions existed, etc.

2. Mark and label smaller maps of continents to illustrate more specific locations, for example, when making a "who, what, when, where" Foldable.

3. Hundreds grids can be used to illustrate percentages, decimals, and bar graphs.

4. Use time lines to record when someone lived or when an event or sequence of events occurred. Use two parallel time lines to compare what was happening in two different areas at the same time.

5. Use small picture frames to sketch or name a person, place, or thing. Great to use with the four-door book as a "who, what, when, where" activity.

6. Use rain gauges and thermometers in projects to record average precipitation amounts or average seasonal temperatures of a geographic area.

> **NOTE**: *I grant you permission to photocopy these pages and place copies of them in the production center or publishing center of your classroom. I also grant you permission to scan these pages and use them electronically.*

National Social Studies Standards and Communication Skills

The National Social Studies Standards stress the importance of communication skills in social studies education. Not all students will become government officials, geographers, or historians, but all students need to be able to think, analyze, and communicate using social studies skills. Throughout their lives, students will be called upon to be literate in social studies as they make observations, analyze and recall empirical data, read and differentiate between fact and opinion, discuss pros and cons of actions and reactions, justify voting for or against an issue, research a topic related to their well-being or interests, make cause-and-effect decisions about their actions, write letters to the editor to express their views publicly, and more. Foldables are one of many techniques that can be used to integrate reading, writing, thinking, debating, researching, and other communication skills into an interdisciplinary social studies curriculum.

Basic Foldable Shapes

The following figures illustrate the basic folds that are referred to throughout the following section of this book.

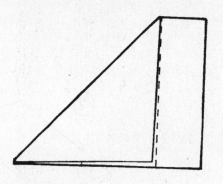

Taco Fold

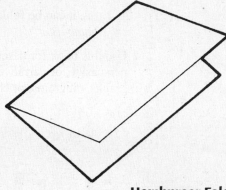

Hamburger Fold

Hot Dog Fold

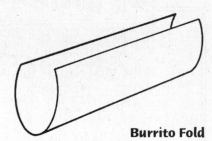

Burrito Fold

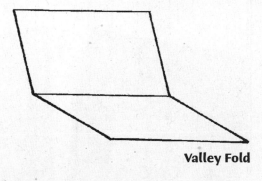

Valley Fold

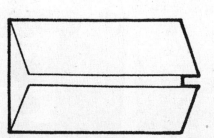

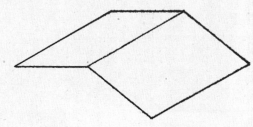

Shutter Fold

Mountain Fold

Half-Book

Fold a sheet of paper (8 1/2" x 11") in half.

1. This book can be folded vertically like a *hot dog* or . . .

2. . . . it can be folded horizontally like a *hamburger*.

Use this book for descriptive, expository, persuasive, or narrative writing, as well as for graphs, diagrams, or charts.

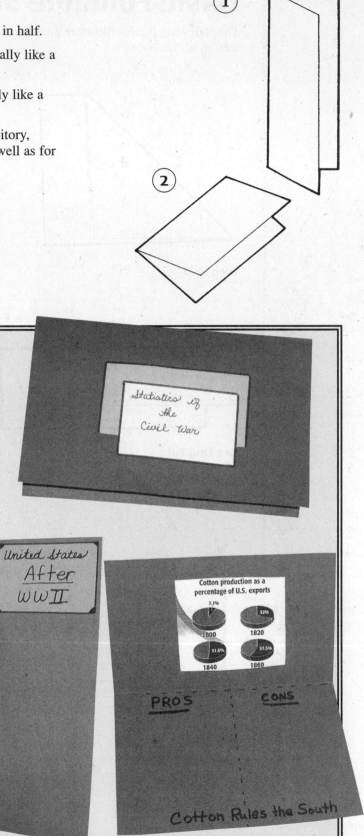

Folded Book

1. Make a *half-book*.

2. Fold it in half again like a *hamburger*. This produces a ready-made cover, and two small pages for information on the inside.

Use photocopied work sheets, Internet printouts, and student-drawn diagrams or maps to create this book. One sheet of paper becomes two activities and two grades.

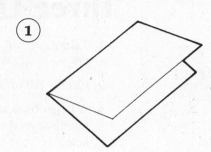

①

②

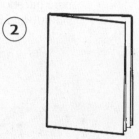

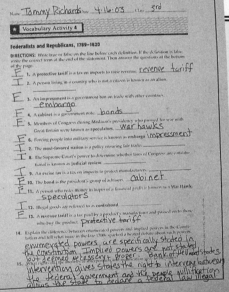

When folded, the worksheet becomes a book for recording notes and questions.

Three-Quarter Book

1. Take a *two-tab* book and raise the left-hand tab.

2. Cut the tab off at the top fold line.

3. A larger book of information can be made by gluing several *three-quarter books* side-by-side.

Sketch or glue a graphic to the left, write one or more questions on the right, and record answers and information under the right tab.

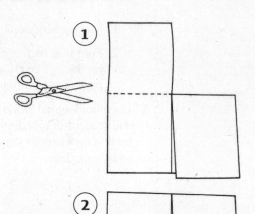

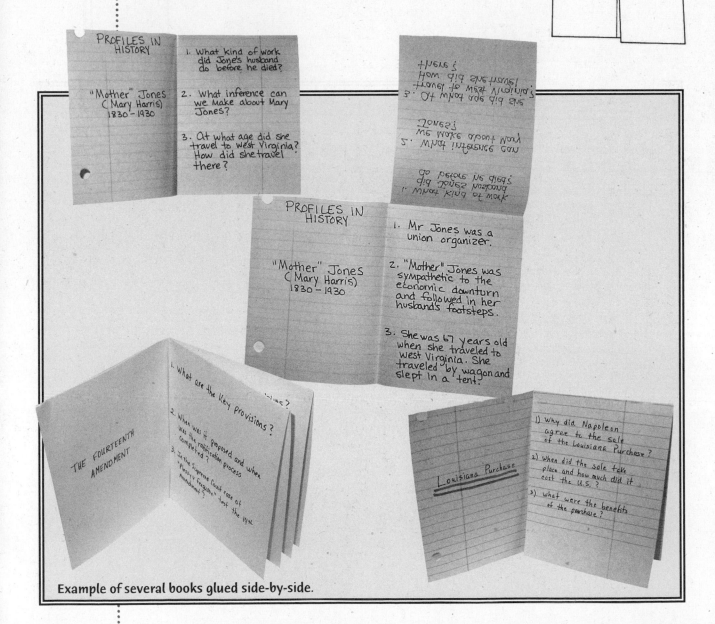

Example of several books glued side-by-side.

Bound Book

1. Take two sheets of paper (8 1/2" x 11") and separately fold them like a *hamburger*. Place the papers on top of each other, leaving one-sixteenth of an inch between the *mountain tops*.

2. Mark both folds one inch from the outer edges.

3. On one of the folded sheets, cut from the top and bottom edge to the marked spot on both sides.

4. On the second folded sheet, start at one of the marked spots and cut the fold between the two marks.

5. Take the cut sheet from step 3 and fold it like a *burrito*. Place the *burrito* through the other sheet and then open the *burrito*. Fold the bound pages in half to form an eight-page book.

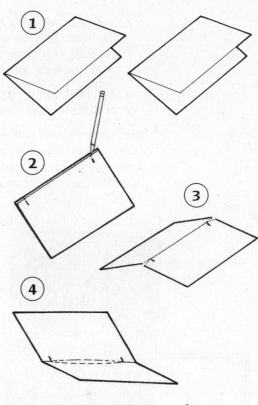

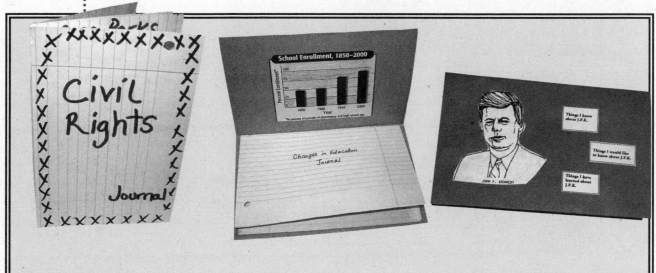

Two-Tab Book

1. Take a *folded book* and cut up the *valley* of the inside fold toward the *mountain top*. This cut forms two large tabs that can be used front and back for writing and illustrations.

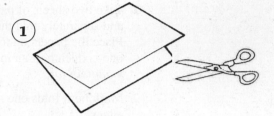

2. The book can be expanded by making several of these folds and gluing them side-by-side.

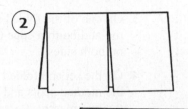

Use this book with data occurring in twos. For example, use it for comparing and contrasting, determining cause and effect, finding similarities and differences, and more.

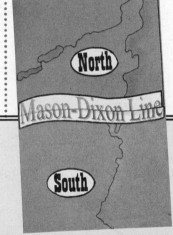

North

Mason-Dixon Line

South

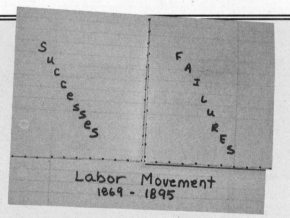

Successes

Failures

Labor Movement
1869 - 1895

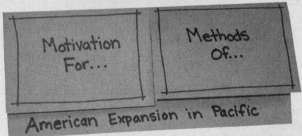

Motivation For...

Methods Of...

American Expansion in Pacific

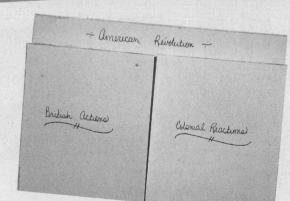

~ American Revolution ~

British Actions

Colonial Reactions

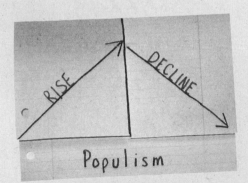

RISE

DECLINE

Populism

Pocket Book

1. Fold a sheet of paper (8 1/2" x 11") in half like a *hamburger*.

2. Open the folded paper and fold one of the long sides up two inches to form a pocket. Refold along the *hamburger* fold so that the newly formed pockets are on the inside.

3. Glue the outer edges of the two-inch fold with a small amount of glue.

4. Optional: Glue a cover around the *pocket book*.

Variation: Make a multi-paged booklet by gluing several pockets side-by-side. Glue a cover around the multi-paged *pocket book*.

Use 3" x 5" index cards inside the pockets. Store student-made books, such as two-tab books and folded books in the pockets.

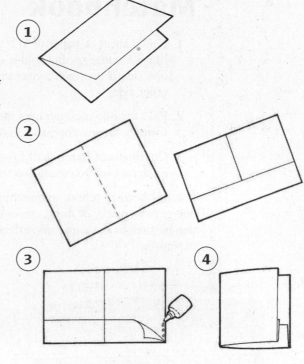

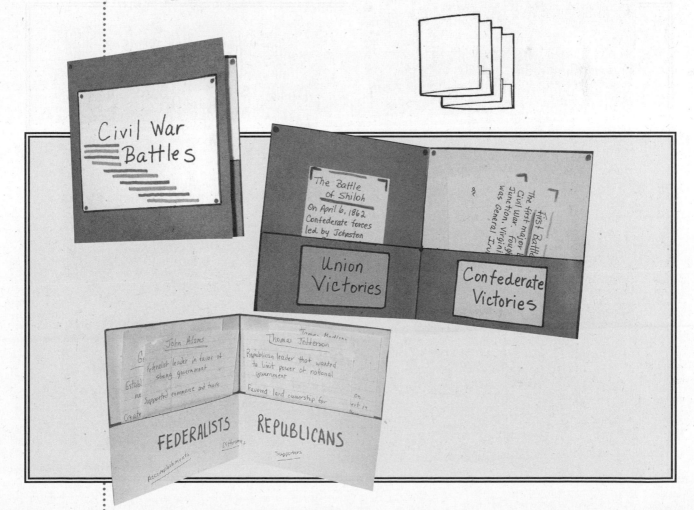

Matchbook

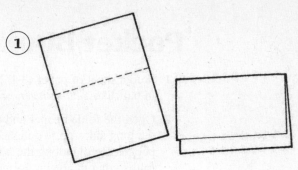

1. Fold a sheet of paper (8 1/2" x 11") like a *hamburger,* but fold it so that one side is one inch longer than the other side.

2. Fold the one-inch tab over the short side forming an envelope-like fold.

3. Cut the front flap in half toward the *mountain top* to create two flaps.

Use this book to report on one thing, such as one person, place, or thing, or for reporting on two things, such as the cause and effect of Western expansion.

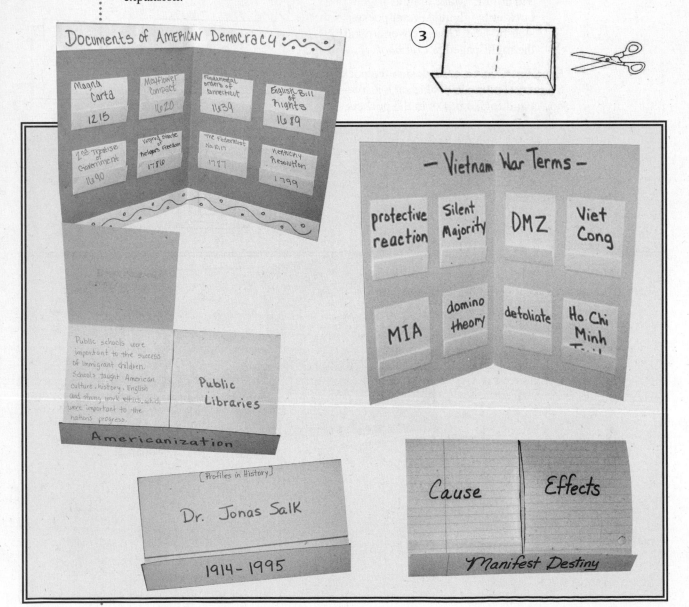

Shutter Fold

1. Begin as if you were going to make a *hamburger* but instead of creasing the paper, pinch it to show the midpoint.

2. Fold the outer edges of the paper to meet at the pinch, or mid-point, forming a *shutter fold*.

Use this book for data occurring in twos. Or, make this fold using 11" x 17" paper and smaller books—such as the half book, journal, and two-tab book—that can be glued inside to create a large project full of student work.

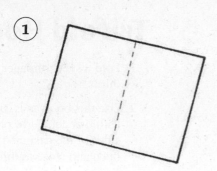

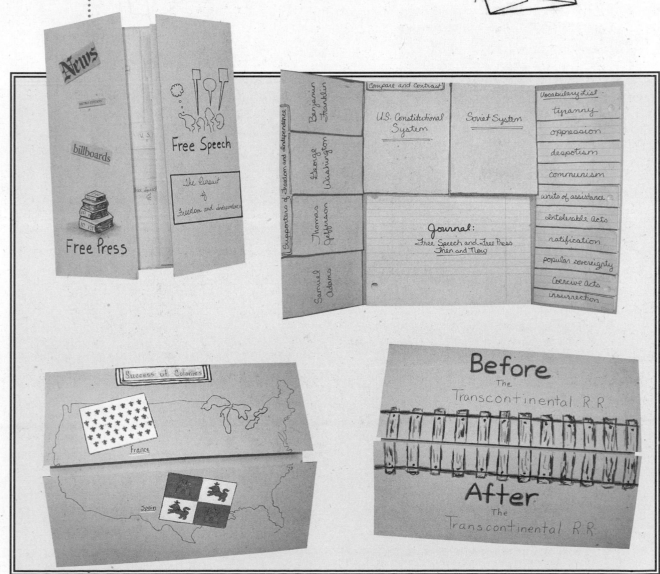

Trifold Book

1. Fold a sheet of paper (8 1/2" x 11") into thirds.

2. Use this book as is, or cut into shapes. If the trifold is cut, leave plenty of fold on both sides of the designed shape, so the book will open and close in three sections.

Use this book to make charts with three columns or rows, large Venn diagrams, reports on data occurring in threes, or to show the outside and inside of something and to write about it.

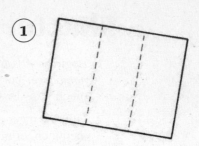

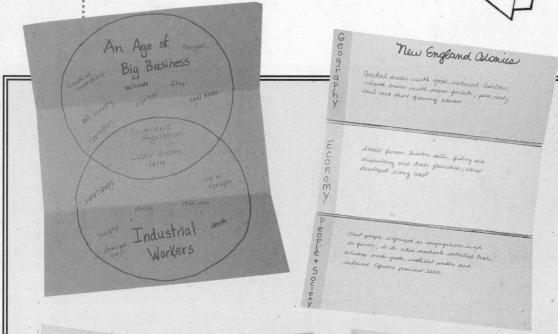

Three-Tab Book

1. Fold a sheet of paper like a *hot dog*.

2. With the paper horizontal, and the fold of the *hot dog* up, fold the right side toward the center, trying to cover one half of the paper.

   NOTE: *If you fold the right edge over first, the final graphic organizer will open and close like a book.*

3. Fold the left side over the right side to make a book with three folds.

4. Open the folded book. Place your hands between the two thicknesses of paper and cut up the two *valleys* on one side only. This will form three tabs.

Use this book for data occurring in threes, and for two-part Venn diagrams.

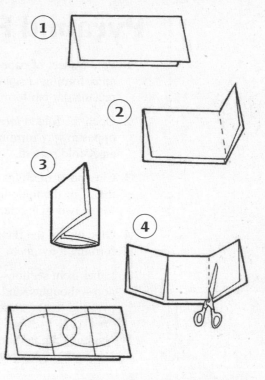

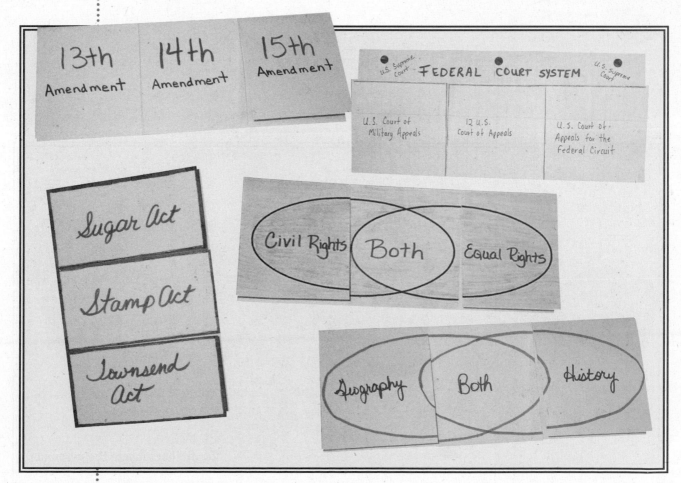

Pyramid Fold

1. Fold a sheet of paper (8 1/2" x 11") into a *taco,* forming a square. Cut off the excess rectangular tab formed by the fold.

2. Open the folded *taco* and refold it the opposite way forming another *taco* and an X-fold pattern.

3. Cut one of the folds to the center of the X, or the midpoint, and stop. This forms two triangular-shaped flaps.

4. Glue one of the flaps under the other, forming a *pyramid.*

5. Label front sections and write information, notes, thoughts, and questions inside the pyramid on the back of the appropriate tab.

Use to make mobiles and dioramas.
Use with data occurring in threes.

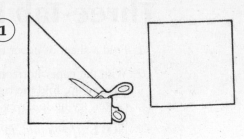

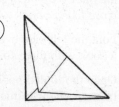

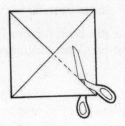

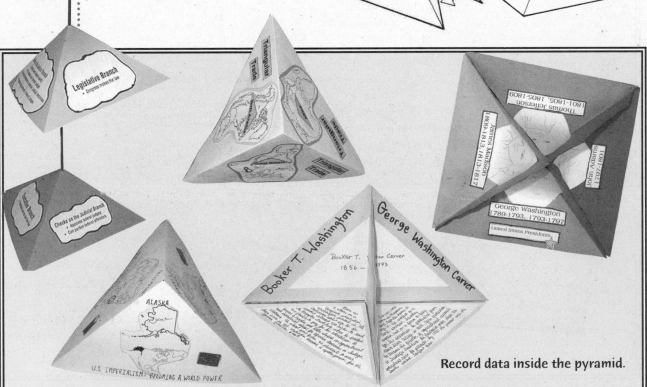

Record data inside the pyramid.

Layered-Look Book

1. Stack two sheets of paper (8 1/2" x 11") so that the back sheet is one inch higher than the front sheet.

2. Bring the bottom of both sheets upward and align the edges so that all of the layers or tabs are the same distance apart.

3. When all tabs are an equal distance apart, fold the papers and crease well.

4. Open the papers and glue them together along the *valley* or inner center fold or, staple them along the *mountain*.

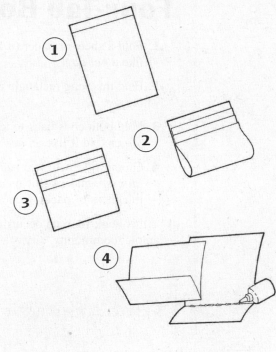

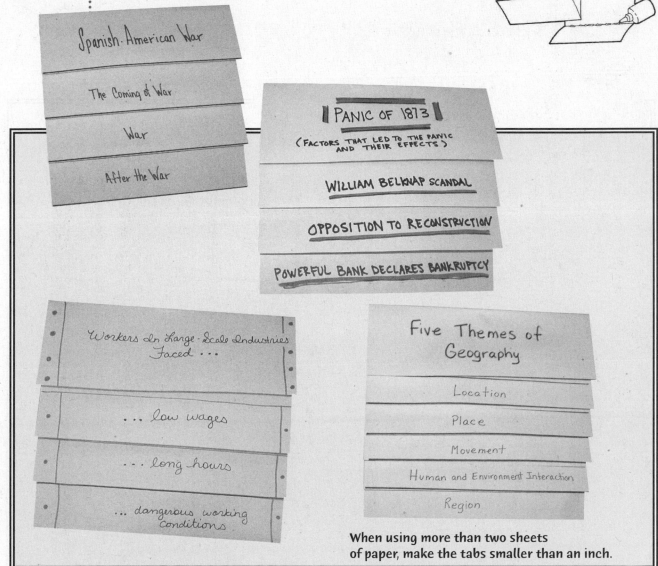

Spanish-American War

The Coming of War

War

After the War

PANIC OF 1873
(FACTORS THAT LED TO THE PANIC AND THEIR EFFECTS)

WILLIAM BELKNAP SCANDAL

OPPOSITION TO RECONSTRUCTION

POWERFUL BANK DECLARES BANKRUPTCY

Workers In Large-Scale Industries Faced . . .

. . . low wages

. . . long hours

. . . dangerous working conditions

Five Themes of Geography

Location

Place

Movement

Human and Environment Interaction

Region

When using more than two sheets of paper, make the tabs smaller than an inch.

Four-Tab Book

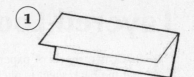

1. Fold a sheet of paper (8 1/2" x 11") in half like a *hot dog*.

2. Fold this long rectangle in half like a *hamburger*.

3. Fold both ends back to touch the *mountain top* or fold it like an *accordion*.

4. On the side with two *valleys* and one *mountain top,* make vertical cuts through one thickness of paper, forming four tabs.

Use this book for data occurring in fours. For example: community, city, state, and nation.

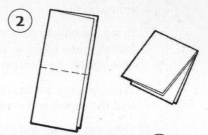
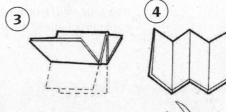
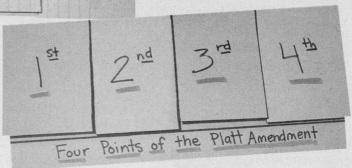

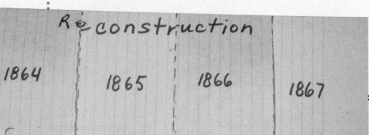

Reconstruction

1864   1865   1866   1867

1st   2nd   3rd   4th

Four Points of the Platt Amendment

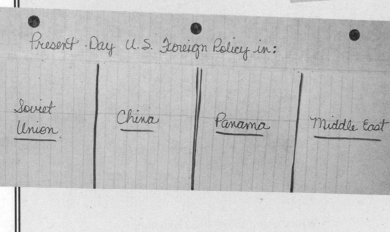

Present Day U.S. Foreign Policy in:

Soviet Union   China   Panama   Middle East

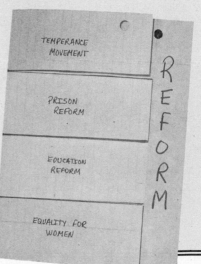

TEMPERANCE MOVEMENT

PRISON REFORM

EDUCATION REFORM

EQUALITY FOR WOMEN

R E F O R M

Standing Cube

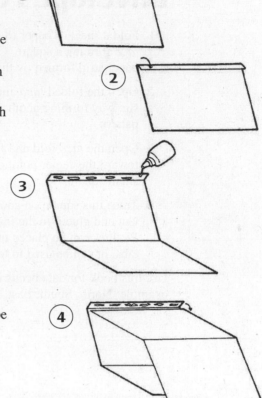

1. Use two sheets of the same size paper. Fold each like a *hamburger,* but, fold one side one half inch shorter than the other. This will make a tab that extends out one half inch on one side.

2. Fold the long side over the short side of both sheets of paper, making tabs.

3. On one of the folded papers, place a small amount of glue along the the small folded tab, next to the *valley* but not in it.

4. Place the non-folded edge of the second sheet of paper square into the *valley* and fold the glue-covered tab over this sheet of paper. Press flat until the glue holds. Repeat with the other side.

5. Allow the glue to dry completely before continuing. After the glue has dried, the cube can be collapsed flat to allow students to work at their desks. The cube can also be folded into fourths for easier storage, or for moving it to a display area.

Use with data occurring in fours or make it into a project. Make a small display cube using 8 1/2" x 11" paper. Use 11" x 17" paper to make large project cubes that you can glue other books onto for display. Notebook paper, photocopied sheets, magazine pictures, and current events also can be displayed on the large cube.

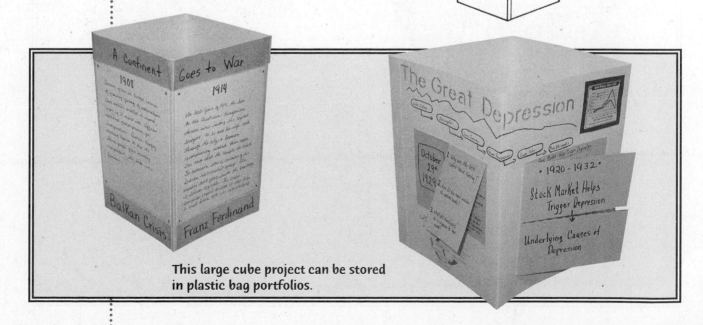

This large cube project can be stored in plastic bag portfolios.

Envelope Fold

1. Fold a sheet of paper (8 1/2" x 11") into a *taco* forming a square. Cut off the excess paper strip formed by the square.

2. Open the folded *taco* and refold it the opposite way forming another *taco* and an X fold pattern.

3. Open the *taco* fold and fold the corners toward the center point of the X forming a small square.

4. Trace this square on another sheet of paper. Cut and glue it to the inside of the envelope. Pictures can be placed under or on top of the tabs, or can be used to teach fractional parts.

Use this book for data occurring in fours. For example: North, South, East, and West

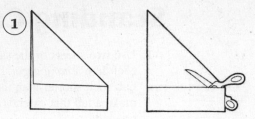

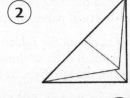

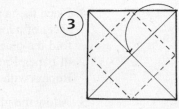

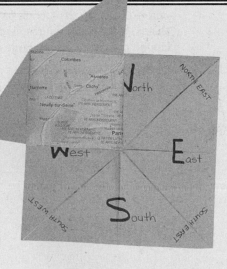

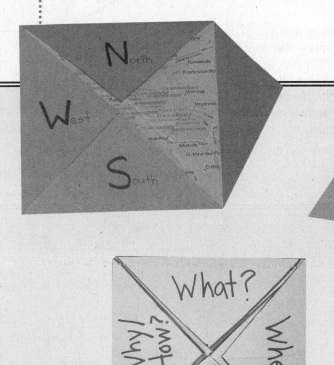

Four-Door Book

1. Make a *shutter fold* using 11" x 17" or 12" x 18" paper.

2. Fold the *shutter fold* in half like a *hamburger.* Crease well.

3. Open the project and cut along the two inside *valley* folds.

4. These cuts will form four doors on the inside of the project.

Use this fold for data occurring in fours. When folded in half like a *hamburger,* a finished *four-door book* can be glued inside a large (11" x 17") *shutter fold* as part of a larger project.

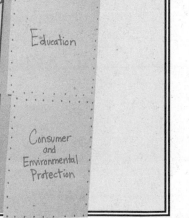

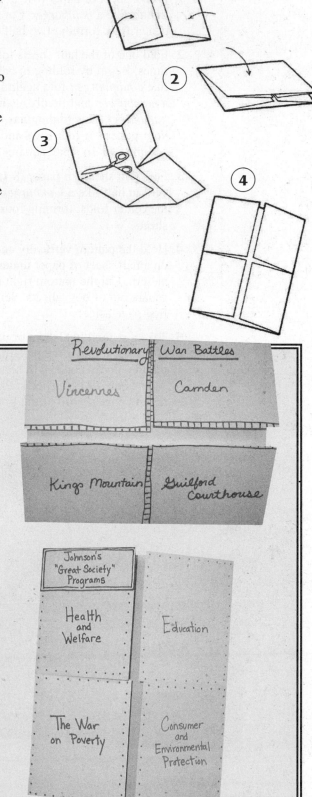

Top-Tab Book

1. Fold a sheet of paper (8 1/2" x 11") in half like a *hamburger*. Cut the center fold, forming two half sheets.

2. Fold one of the half sheets four times. Begin by folding in half like a *hamburger*, fold again like a *hamburger*, and finally again like a *hamburger*. This folding has formed your pattern of four rows and four columns, or 16 small squares.

3. Fold two sheets of paper (8 1/2" x 11") in half like a *hamburger*. Cut the center folds, forming four half sheets.

4. Hold the pattern vertically and place on a half sheet of paper under the pattern. Cut the bottom right hand square out of both sheets. Set this first page aside.

5. Take a second half sheet of paper and place it under the pattern. Cut the first and second right hand squares out of both sheets. Place the second page on top of the first page.

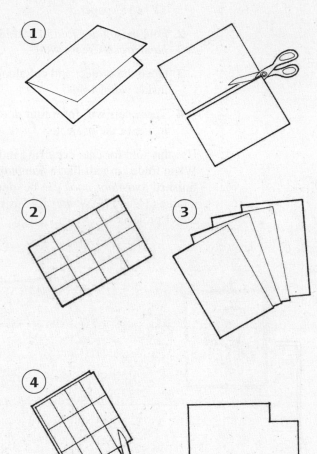

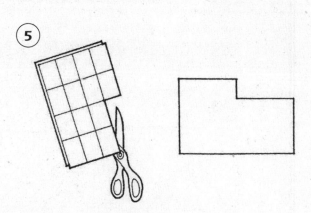

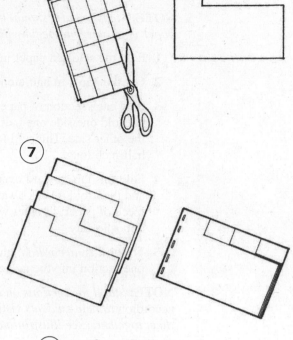

6. Take a third half sheet of paper and place it under the pattern. Cut the first, second, and third right hand squares out of both sheets. Place this third page on top of the second page.

7. Place the fourth, uncut half sheet of paper behind the three cut out sheets, leaving four aligned tabs across the top of the book. Staple several times on the left side. You can also place glue along the left paper edges, and stack them together. The glued spine is very strong.

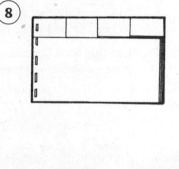

8. Cut a final half sheet of paper with no tabs and staple along the left side to form a cover.

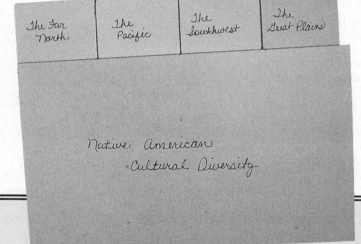

Accordion Book

NOTE: *Steps 1 and 2 should be done only if paper is too large to begin with.*

1. Fold the selected paper into *hamburgers*.

2. Cut the paper in half along the fold lines.

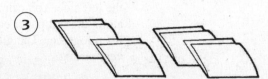

3. Fold each section of paper into *hamburgers*, but fold one side one half inch shorter than the other side. This will form a tab that is one half inch long.

4. Fold this tab forward over the shorter side, and then fold it back away from the shorter piece of paper; in other words, fold it the opposite way.

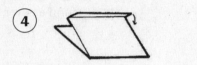

5. To form an *accordion*, glue a straight edge of one section into the *valley* of another section.

NOTE: *Stand the sections on end to form an accordion to help students visualize how to glue them together. (See illustration.)*

Always place the extra tab at the back of the book so you can add more pages later.

Use this book for time lines, student projects that grow, sequencing events or data, and biographies.

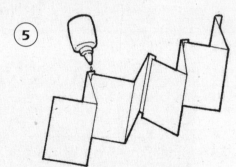

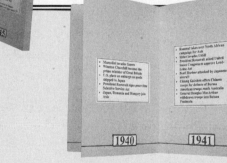

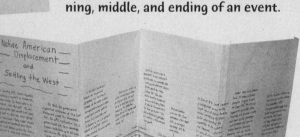

Use different colored paper to indicate before and after, or the beginning, middle, and ending of an event.

When folded, this project is used like a book, and it can be stored in student portfolios. When open, it makes a nice project display. Accordion books can be stored in file cabinets for future use, too.

Pop-Up Book

1. Fold a sheet of paper (8 1/2" x 11") in half like a *hamburger*.

2. Beginning at the fold, or *mountain* top, cut one or more tabs.

3. Fold the tabs back and forth several times until there is a good fold line formed.

4. Partially open the *hamburger* fold and push the tabs through to the inside.

5. With one small dot of glue, glue figures for the *pop-up book* to the front of each tab. Allow the glue to dry before going on to the next step.

6. Make a cover for the book by folding another sheet of paper in half like a *hamburger*. Place glue around the outside edges of the *pop-up book* and firmly press inside the *hamburger* cover.

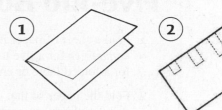

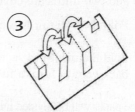

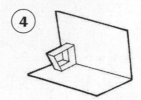

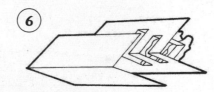

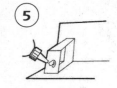

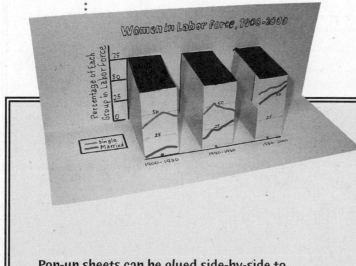

Pop-up sheets can be glued side-by-side to make pop-up books.

Five-Tab Book

1. Fold a sheet of paper in half like a *hot dog* or *hamburger* for a five tab book, or leave open for a folded table or chart.

2. Fold the paper so that one third is exposed and two thirds are covered.

3. Fold the two thirds section in half.

4. Fold the one third section (single thickness) backward to form a fold line.

The paper will be divided into fifths when opened

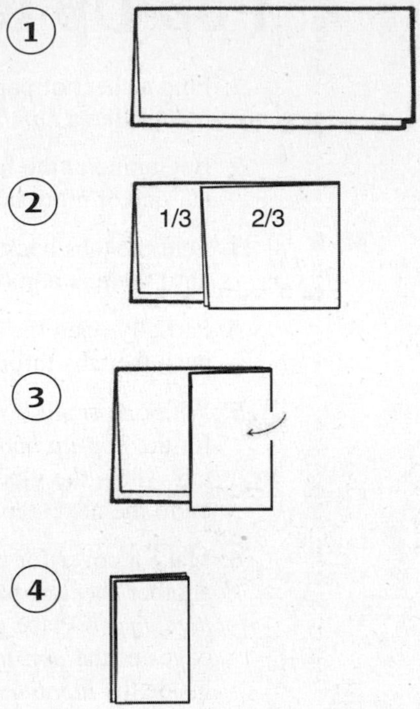

①

② 1/3 | 2/3

③

④

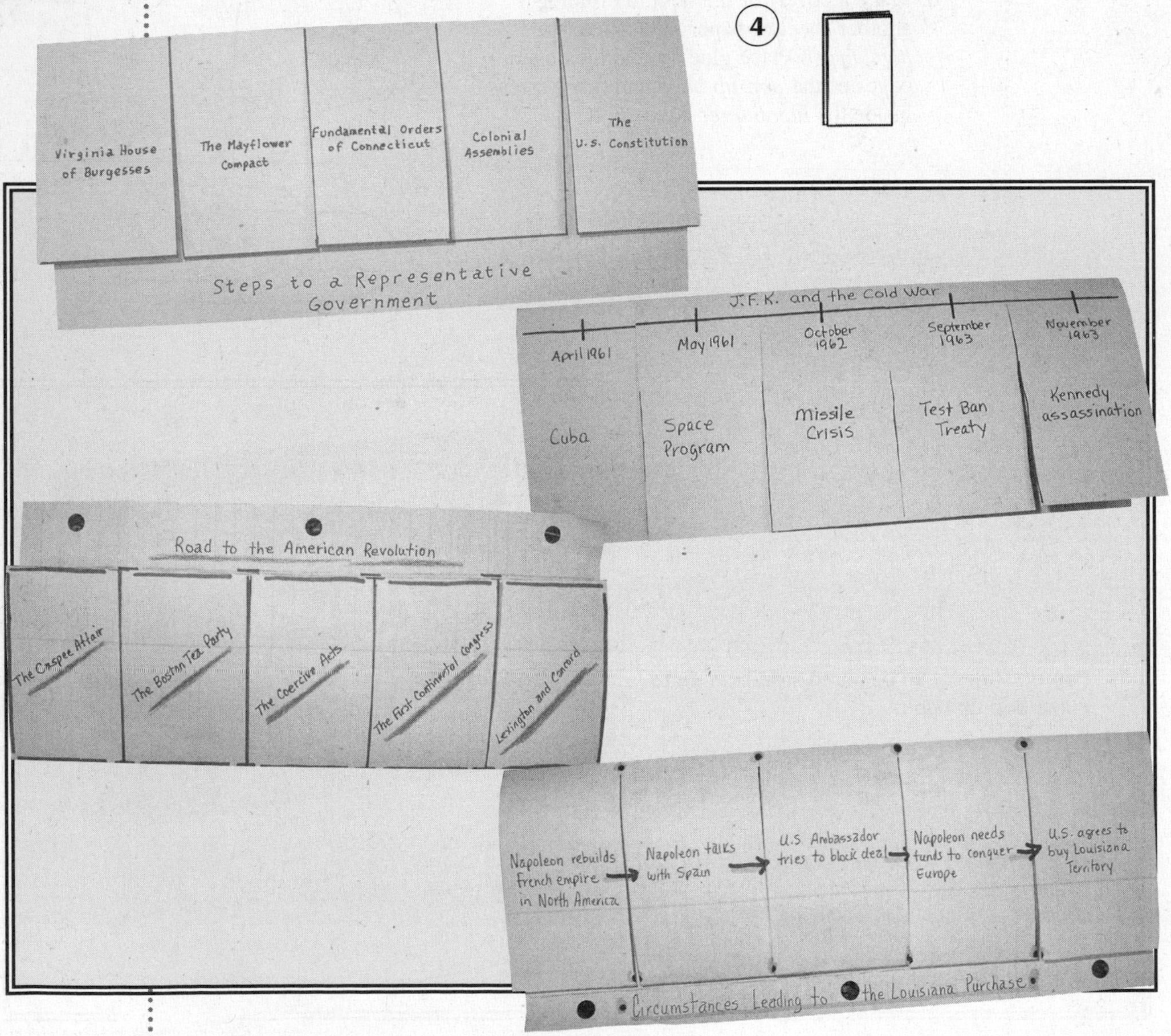

Virginia House of Burgesses | The Mayflower Compact | Fundamental Orders of Connecticut | Colonial Assemblies | The U.S. Constitution

Steps to a Representative Government

J.F.K. and the Cold War

April 1961 | May 1961 | October 1962 | September 1963 | November 1963

Cuba | Space Program | Missile Crisis | Test Ban Treaty | Kennedy assassination

Road to the American Revolution

The Gaspee Affair | The Boston Tea Party | The Coercive Acts | The First Continental Congress | Lexington and Concord

Napoleon rebuilds French empire in North America → Napoleon talks with Spain → U.S Ambassador tries to block deal → Napoleon needs funds to conquer Europe → U.S. agrees to buy Louisiana Territory

Circumstances Leading to the Louisiana Purchase

Folded Table or Chart

1. Fold the number of vertical columns needed to make the table or chart.

2. Fold the horizontal rows needed to make the table or chart.

3. Label the rows and columns.

Remember: Tables are organized along vertical and horizontal axes, while charts are organized along one axis, either horizontal or vertical.

Table

Chart

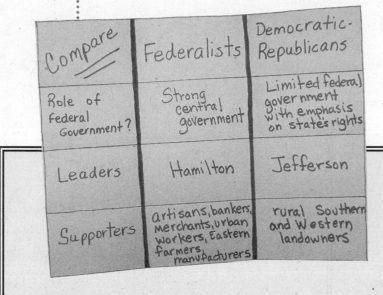

Compare	Federalists	Democratic-Republicans
Role of federal Government?	Strong central government	Limited federal government with emphasis on state's rights
Leaders	Hamilton	Jefferson
Supporters	Artisans, bankers, merchants, urban workers, Eastern farmers, manufacturers	rural Southern and Western landowners

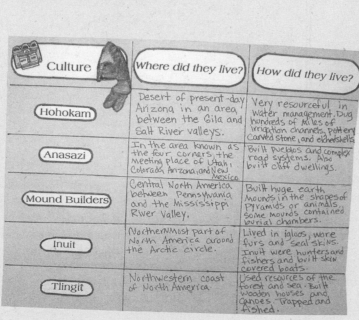

Culture	Where did they live?	How did they live?
Hohokam	Desert of present-day Arizona in an area between the Gila and Salt River valleys.	Very resourceful in water management. Dug hundreds of miles of irrigation channels. Pottery, carved stone, and etched shells.
Anasazi	In the area known as the four corners, the meeting place of Utah, Colorado, Arizona, and New Mexico.	Built pueblos and complex road systems. Also built cliff dwellings.
Mound Builders	Central North America between Pennsylvania and the Mississippi River Valley.	Built huge earth mounds in the shapes of pyramids or animals. Some mounds contained burial chambers.
Inuit	Northernmost part of North America around the Arctic circle.	Lived in igloos, wore furs and seal skins. Inuit were hunters and fishers and built skin covered boats.
Tlingit	Northwestern coast of North America.	Used resources of the forest and sea. Built wooden houses and canoes. Trapped and fished.

Explorer	Region	Date
Christopher Columbus	Caribbean Islands, Central American Coast, N. South America	1492-1504
Amerigo Vespucci	N. South America, Caribbean Islands	1499-1500
Pedro Cabral	South America	1500
John Cabot	North America	1497-1498
Martin Frobisher	Between North America and Greenland	1576-1578
Giovanni da Verrazano	North America, Newfoundland	1524
Jacques Cartier	Newfoundland, North America	1534
Henry Hudson	Scandinavia, Newfoundland, North America	1609

Folding a Circle Into Tenths

1. Fold a paper circle in half.

2. Fold the half circle so that one third is exposed and two thirds are covered.

3. Fold the one third (single thickness) backward to form a fold line.

4. Fold the two thirds section in half.

5. The half circle will be divided into fifths. When opened, the circle will be divided into tenths.

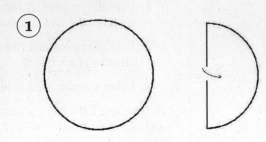

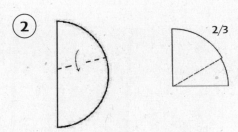

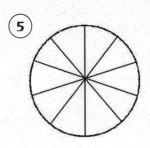

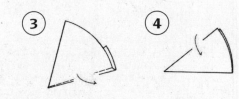

NOTE: *Paper squares and rectangles are folded into tenths the same way. Fold them so that one third is exposed and two thirds is covered. Continue with steps 3 and 4.*

Circle Graph

1. Cut out two circles using a pattern.

2. Fold one of the circles in half on each axis, forming fourths. Cut along one of the fold lines (the radius) to the middle of each circle. Flatten the circle.

3. Slip the two circles together along the cuts until they overlap completely.

4. Spin one of the circles while holding the other stationary. Estimate how much of each of the two (or you can add more) circles should be exposed to illustrate given percentages or fractional parts of data. Add circles to represent more than two percentages.

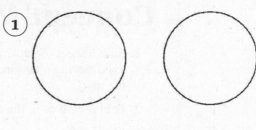

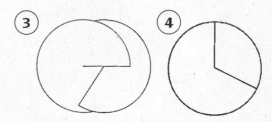

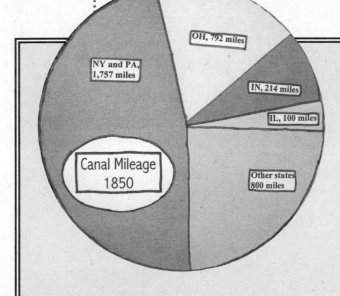

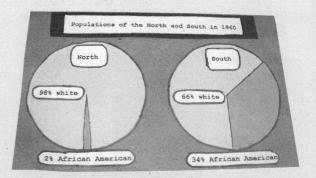

Use large circle graphs on bulletin boards.

Use small circle graphs in student projects or on the front of tab books.

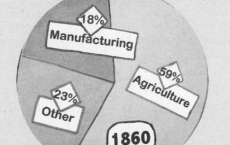

Concept-Map Book

1. Fold a sheet of paper along the long or short axis, leaving a two-inch tab uncovered along the top.

2. Fold in half or in thirds.

3. Unfold and cut along the two or three inside fold lines.

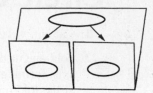

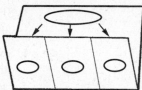

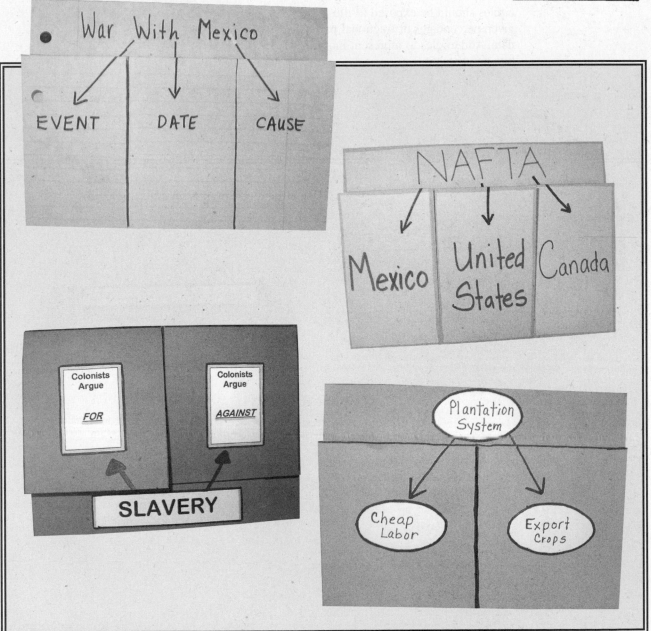

Vocabulary Book

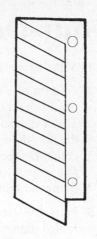

1. Fold a sheet of notebook paper in half like a *hotdog*.

2. On one side, cut every third line. This results in ten tabs on wide ruled notebook paper and twelve tabs on college ruled.

3. Label the tabs.

U.S. Constitution Vocabulary List

Relinquish

Annihilation

Convulsions

Tenure

Quartering

Render

Abdicated

Insurrections

Unwarrantable jurisdiction

Consanguinity

Use for vocabulary books.

Amendments

Guarantees freedom of religion, speech, assembly, and press, and the right of the people to petition the government.

2

3

4

5

6

7

8

9

10

Bill of Rights

Use to take notes and record data. Leave the notebook holes uncovered and it can be stored in a notebook.

Questions and Answers

1. How did Microsoft differ from other computer companies?

2. How did deregulation affect the telecommunications industry?

3. How did the Internet expand business opportunities?

4. Why did President Clinton's proposed health care plan fail?

5. What two reforms did Clinton and Congress agree to support?

6. What events led to the impeachment of Clinton?

7. Why was the European Union (EU) created in 1993?

8. What was President G.W. Bush's first priority when he took office?

9. What are the three main reasons certain Muslims became angry with the U.S.?

10. How did Americans respond to the 9/11 attacks?

Use for recording student questions and answers.

Four-Door Diorama

1. Make a *four-door book* out of a *shutter fold*.

2. Fold the two inside corners back to the outer edges (*mountains*) of the *shutter fold*. This will result in two *tacos* that will make the *four-door book* look like it has a shirt collar. Do the same thing to the bottom of the *four-door book*. When finished, four small triangular *tacos* have been made.

3. Form a 90-degree angle and overlap the folded triangles to make a display case that doesn't use staples or glue. (It can be collapsed for storage.)

4. Or, as illustrated, cut off all four triangles, or *tacos*. Staple or glue the sides.

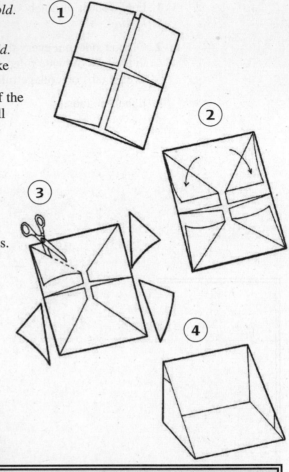

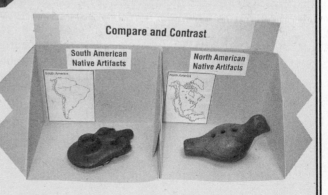

Use 11" x 17" paper to make a large display case.

Use poster board to make giant display cases.

Glue display cases end-to-end to compare and contrast or to sequence events or data.

Picture-Frame Book

1. Fold a sheet of paper (8 1/2" x 11") in half like a *hamburger*.

2. Open the *hamburger* and gently roll one side of the *hamburger* toward the *valley*. Try not to crease the roll.

3. Cut a rectangle out of the middle of the rolled side of the paper leaving a half-inch border, forming a frame.

4. Fold another sheet of paper (8 1/2" x 11") in half like a *hamburger*. Apply glue to the inside border of the picture frame and place the folded, uncut sheet of paper inside.

Use this book to feature a person, place, or thing. Inside the picture frames, glue photographs, magazine pictures, computer-generated graphs, or have students sketch pictures. This book has three inside pages for writing and recording notes.

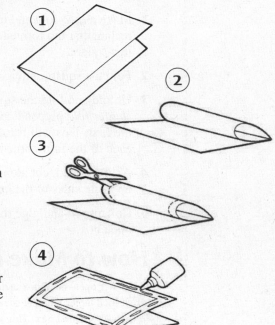

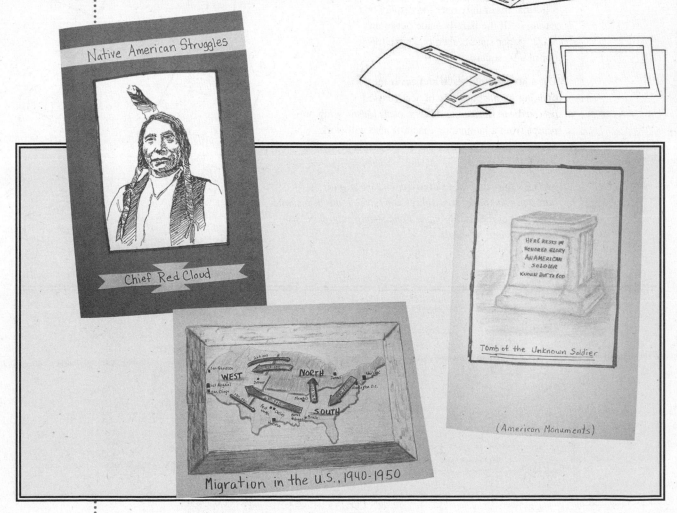

Native American Struggles

Chief Red Cloud

Migration in the U.S., 1940-1950

HERE RESTS IN HONORED GLORY AN AMERICAN SOLDIER KNOWN BUT TO GOD

Tomb of the Unknown Soldier

(American Monuments)

Display Case

1. Make a *taco* fold and cut off the rectangular tab formed. This will result in a square.

2. Fold the square into a *shutter fold*.

3. Unfold and fold the square into another *shutter fold* perpendicular to the direction of the first. This will form a small square at each of the four corners of the sheet of paper.

4. As illustrated, cut along two fold lines on opposite sides of the large square.

5. Collapse in and glue the cut tabs to form an open box.

How to Make a Lid

Fold another open-sided box using a square of paper one-half inch larger than the square used to make the first box. This will make a lid that fits snugly over the display box. *Example:* If the base is made out of an 8 1/2" paper square, then make the top out of a 9" square.

Cut a hole out of the lid and cover the opening with a cut piece of acetate used on overhead projectors. Heavy, clear plastic wrap or scraps from a laminating machine also will work. Secure the clear plastic sheet to the inside of the lid with glue or tape.

NOTE: *You can place polystyrene foam or quilt batting in the boxes to display insects. Glue the boxes onto a sheet of cardboard to make them strong enough to display rocks and minerals.*

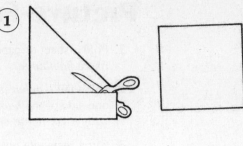

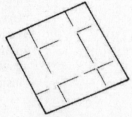

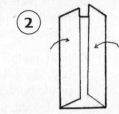

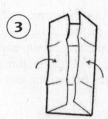

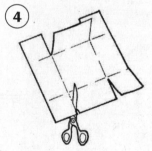

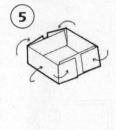

U.S. AIR FORCE
BRONZE STAR MEDAL

LIBERTY STANDING
HALF DOLLAR (Silver)
SCARCE
1939-S $3.50

RARE U.S. CURRENCY

Billboard Project

1. Fold all pieces of the same size of paper in half like *hamburgers*.

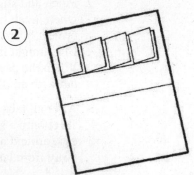

2. Place a line of glue at the top and bottom of one side of each folded billboard section and glue them edge-to-edge on a background paper or project board. If glued correctly, all doors will open from right to left.

3. Pictures, dates, and text go on the front of each billboard section. When opened, writing or drawings can be seen on the inside left of each section. The base, or the part glued to the background, is perfect for in-depth information or definitions.

Use for time lines or sequencing data, such as events in a war, presidents of the United States, or ratification of states.

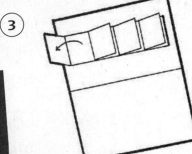

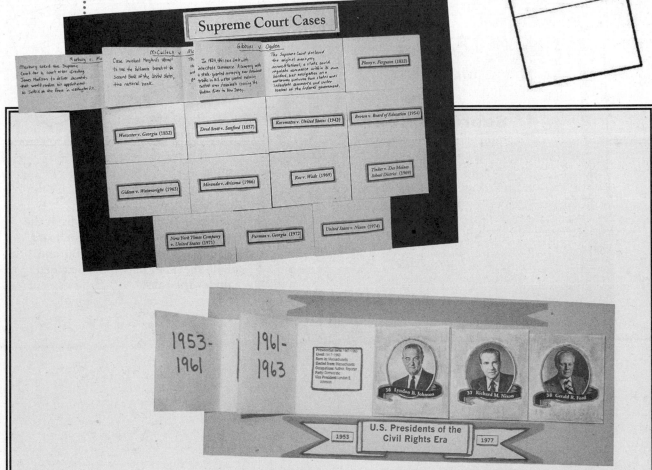

Project Board with Tabs

1. Draw a large illustration or a series of small illustrations or write on the front of one of the pieces of selected-size paper.

2. Pinch and slightly fold the paper at the point where a tab is desired on the illustrated project board. Cut into the paper on the fold. Cut straight in, then cut up to form an "L." When the paper is unfolded, it will form a tab with an illustration on the front.

3. After all tabs have been cut, glue this front sheet onto a second piece of paper. Place glue around all four edges and in the middle, away from tabs.

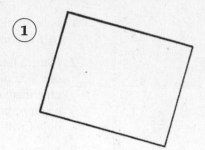

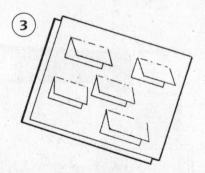

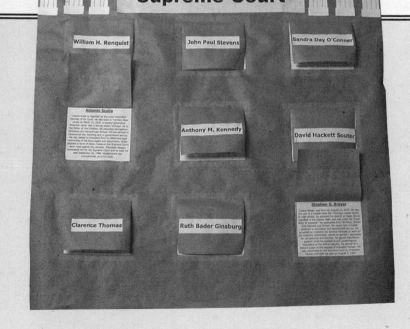

Write or draw under the tabs. If the project is made as a bulletin board using butcher paper, quarter and half-sheets of paper can be glued under the tabs.

Sentence Strips

1. *Take two sheets of paper (8 1/2" x 11") and fold into hamburgers. Cut along the fold lines making four half sheets. (Use as many half sheets as necessary for additional pages to your book.)*

2. Fold each sheet in half like a *hot dog*.

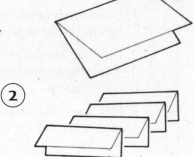

3. Place the folds side-by-side and staple them together on the left side.

4. 1" from the stapled edge, cut the front page of each folded section up to the *mountain top*. These cuts form flaps that can be raised and lowered.

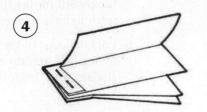

To make a half-cover, use a sheet of construction paper one inch longer than the book. Glue the back of the last sheet to the construction paper strip leaving one inch, on the left side, to fold over and cover the original staples. Staple this half-cover in place.

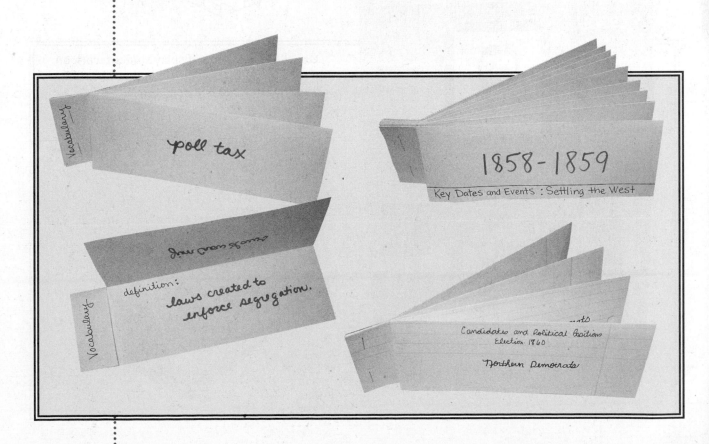

Sentence-Strip Holder

1. Fold a sheet of paper (8 1/2" x 11") in half like a *hamburger*.

2. Open the *hamburger* and fold the two outer edges toward the *valley*. This forms a *shutter fold*.

3. Fold one of the inside edges of the *shutter* back to the outside fold. This fold forms a floppy "L."

4. Glue the floppy L-tab down to the base so that it forms a strong, straight L-tab.

5. Glue the other *shutter* side to the front of this L-tab. This forms a tent that is the backboard for the flashcards or student work to be displayed.

6. Fold the edge of the L-tab up one quarter to one half to form a lip that will keep the student work from slipping off the holder.

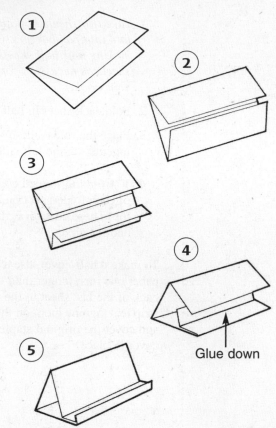

Glue down

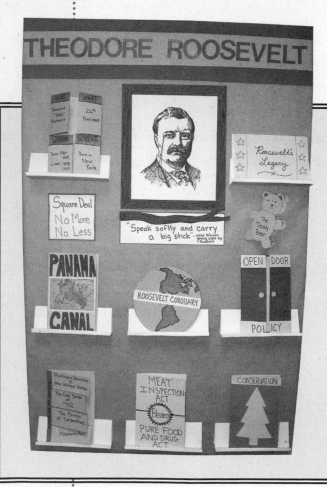

Use these holders to display student work on a table, or glue them onto a bulletin board to make it interactive.

Three-Pocket Book

1. Fold a horizontal sheet of paper (11" x 17") into thirds.

2. Fold the bottom edge up two inches and crease well. Glue the outer edges of the two inch tab to create three pockets.

3. Label each pocket. Use to hold notes taken on index cards or quarter sheets of paper.

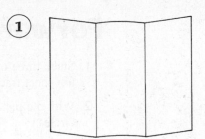

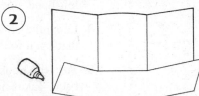

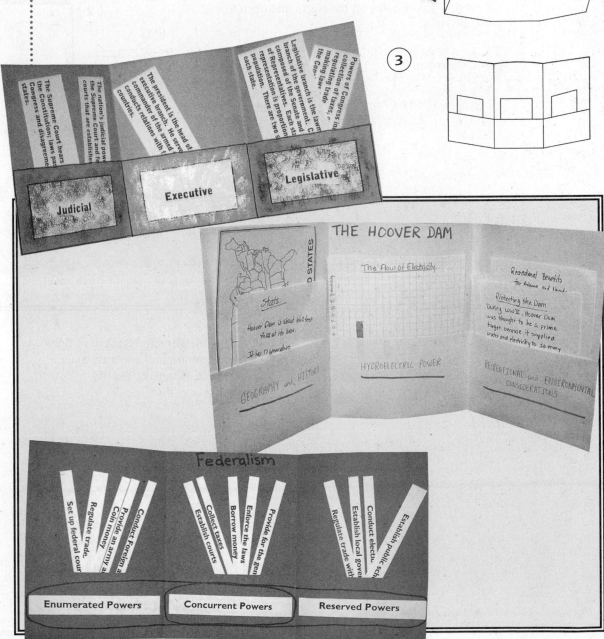

41

Forward-Backward Book

1. Stack three or more sheets of paper. On the top sheet trace a large circle.

2. With the papers still stacked, cut out the circles.

3. Staple the paper circles together along the left-hand side to create a book.

4. Label the cover and takes notes on the pages that open to the right.

5. Turn the book upside down and label the back. Takes notes on the pages that open to the right.

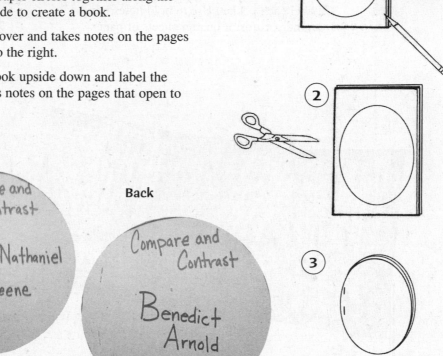

Front

Compare and
Contrast

General Nathaniel
Greene

Back

Compare and
Contrast

Benedict
Arnold

Front

Woman Suffrage
Movement

Susan B. Anthony

Back

Woman Suffrage
Movement

Mary Church Terrell

Use one Forward-Backward book to compare and contrast two people, places, or events.

Activities for

T he pages that follow contain Foldable activities to use for key topics in American government—from important issues in the founding days of the American Republic right through to the present.

For each topic, there is a summary and three Foldable activities, with instructions and illustrations for students. Students review subject material as they create the Foldables. Students can then use their Foldables to prepare for classroom and standardized tests.

CHAPTER I

People and Government

TOPIC SUMMARY

Around the world, people live under a variety of governments. Government exists primarily to maintain social order, provide public services, provide national security, and make economic decisions. All governments also belong to one of three major groups: autocracy—rule by one person; oligarchy—rule by a few persons; or democracy—rule by many people. Finally, governments can be further classified by their economic systems—capitalism, socialism, or communism.

Summarizing the Purposes of Government

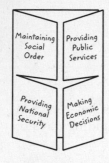

🎧 Four-Door Book

Have students prepare a Four-Door Foldable as a way of summarizing the major purposes of government. The four doors will be labeled as follows: *Maintaining Social Order*, *Providing Public Services*, *Providing National Security*, and *Making Economic Decisions*. Under each of the "doors," students should record examples from the text of the ways in which government accomplishes each task.

Materials Needed: one sheet of 11" x 17" paper, scissors.

Evaluating the Major Types of Government

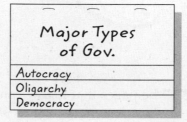

🎧 Layered Book

Students can evaluate the three major types of government—autocracy, oligarchy, and democracy—by creating a Layered Book. Students should define each type of government, give examples of countries with that government in place, and list any other characteristics of each type or sub-type of government.

Materials Needed: two sheets of 8.5" x 11" paper, stapler, or glue.

Analyzing Economic Systems

Economic Systems	History	Economic Decisions
Capitalism		
Socialism		
Communism		

◖ Folded Table

In order to better understand the three major economic systems, have students make a Folded Table. For each type of economic system—capitalism, socialism, and communism—students should note the history of each system in the first column and characteristics of each in the second column.

Materials Needed: one sheet of 11" x 17" paper.

CHAPTER 2

Origins of American Government

TOPIC SUMMARY

During the colonial period, many of the founding principles were formulated that still govern our nation today. The first colonists to arrive in North America drafted and signed the Mayflower Compact as a guide to self-government. Soon, however, tightening British control caused the colonists to rebel and declare independence from Britain. Once independence was won, a new form of self-government was developed and eventually established in the Constitution.

Defining Key Terms

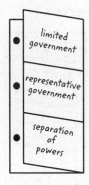

🔊 Vocabulary Book

Have students make a Vocabulary Book to define the key terms from this section. Students should define the following terms: *limited government, representative government,* and *separation of powers.* In addition to defining the terms, students should note the broader context of how each concept contributed to the growth of democracy.

Materials Needed: one sheet of 8.5" x 11" paper, scissors.

Comparing Events in Colonial History

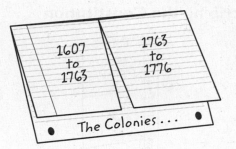

🔊 Two-Tab Book

Have students make a Two-Tab Book to compare the conditions in the colonies during the time periods of 1607 to 1763 and 1763 to 1776. Under each tab, students should note the overall mood of the colonies, their relationship with Britain, and major events that occurred during that time period to change the conditions. This Foldable should help students gain a clear understanding of the events that led to independence.

Materials Needed: one sheet of 8.5" x 11" paper, scissors.

Comparing Governments

	Strengths	Weaknesses
Articles of Confederation		
Constitution		

◖ Folded Table

Students will have a useful tool for comparing the governments formed under the Articles of Confederation and the Constitution by creating this Folded Table. Have students list the strengths and the weaknesses of the government established by each document in the appropriate boxes on the table.

Materials Needed: one sheet of 11" x 17" paper.

CHAPTER 3

The Constitution

TOPIC SUMMARY

The Constitution was created more than 200 years ago to establish a stable government and insure the rights to which all U.S. citizens are entitled. The Constitution establishes three branches of government—the legislative branch, the executive branch, and the judicial branch. These branches work together and provide checks and balances so that no one branch has more power than another. The Constitution may be changed, or amended, under certain circumstances, but still maintains our basic form of government.

Describing the Constitution

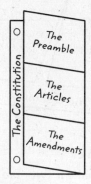

🔖 Three-Tab Book

Students can increase their understanding of the parts of the Constitution with this Three-Tab Foldable. Under each tab, students should describe one of the three parts of the Constitution—*the Preamble*, *the Articles*, and *the Amendments*—using information from the text.

Materials Needed: one sheet of 8.5" x 11" paper, scissors.

Defining Key Terms

🔖 Vocabulary Book

Have students create an Eight-Tab Vocabulary Book. Students should list the following words on one of each of the tabs: *ratify*, *petition*, *balanced budget*, *impeach*, *treaty*, *executive agreement*, *judicial restriction*, and *judicial activism*. On the inside of the tabs, students should write the definition of the word as used in the text.

Materials Needed: one sheet of 8.5" x 11" paper, scissors.

Identifying the Bill of Rights

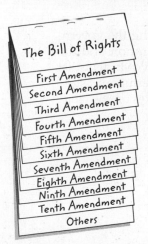

◖ Layered Book

Students will have a handy study guide by creating this Layered Book titled "The Bill of Rights." The tabs for each of the layers will be labeled with the First Amendment through the Tenth Amendment, with one tab left for the other amendments to the Constitution. Inside, students should record a brief description of each amendment and any other facts from the text.

Materials Needed: six sheets of 8.5" x 11" paper, stapler or glue.

CHAPTER 4

The Federal System

TOPIC SUMMARY

The American concept of *federalism*, or the division of government powers, affects everyday decisions at all levels. The Constitution defines the relationship not only between national and state powers, but also between states. For the states, national government must maintain a republican form of government, provide protection from invasion, and maintain territorial integrity. Federalism also requires states to cooperate with each other in many ways.

Defining National Powers

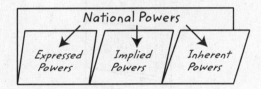

⋂ Three-Tab Concept Map

Have students make a concept map to better understand the three types of national powers. On the front of each tab, students should write *Expressed Powers, Implied Powers,* and *Inherent Powers.* Inside, students can define the term and give examples of each type of power.

Materials Needed: one sheet of 8.5" x 11" paper, scissors.

Summarizing Interstate Relations

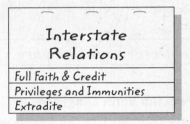

⋂ Layered Book

Students can create a Layered Book to summarize interstate relations. On the first layer, students should summarize the full faith and credit provision of the Constitution. On the second layer, students should explain privileges and immunities. On the third layer, students can explain extradition.

Materials Needed: one sheet of 8.5" x 11" paper.

Debating Federalism

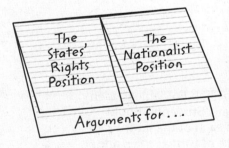

⬅ Two-Tab Book

Ask students to create this Two-Tab Foldable to examine each side of the debate about federalism as presented in the text. On the left side, students should present the arguments for the states' rights position. On the right, they should present the nationalist position.

Materials Needed: one sheet of 8.5" x 11" paper, scissors.

The Organization of Congress

TOPIC SUMMARY

Congress has 535 voting members comprised of 100 senators and 435 representatives. Each congressional member represents a defined geographic area. Citizens of these areas can address issues to their representative in order to be heard. Because the Senate and the House must consider thousands of bills that are proposed to Congress each year, committees and other support staff are used to assist and ease the workload for the congressional representatives.

Describing and Comparing Houses of Congress

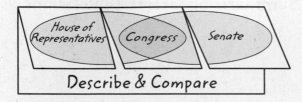

🔊 Three-Tab Venn Diagram

Students can describe and compare the two houses of Congress with a Three-Tab Venn Diagram. On the left tab, students should list the characteristics of the House of Representatives, including qualifications for election and term of office. On the right tab, students should do the same for the Senate. On the center tab, students should list those factors common to both houses of Congress.

Materials Needed: one sheet of 8.5" x 11" paper, scissors.

Identifying House of Representatives Leadership

🔊 Four-Tab Book

Have students make a Four-Tab Foldable to identify the leadership of the House of Representatives. Students should write one of the following on each of the tabs: *Speaker of the House, Majority Leader and Whip, Minority Leader and Whip*, and *The Rules Committee*. Under each tab, students should write a brief description of the responsibilities of each person or group.

Materials Needed: one sheet of 8.5" x 11" paper, scissors.

Identifying Senate Leadership

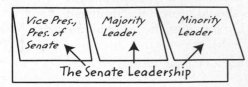

🔊 Three-Tab Book

Have students make a Three-Tab Foldable to identify the leadership of the Senate. Students should write one of the following on each of the tabs: *Vice President/President of the Senate, Majority Leader,* and *Minority Leader*. Under each tab, students should write a brief description of the responsibilities of each person.

Materials Needed: one sheet of 8.5" x 11" paper, scissors.

CHAPTER 6

Development of Congressional Powers

TOPIC SUMMARY

The wording of the Constitution is unclear regarding certain types of powers for either Congress or the president. These implied powers help Congress to expand its role to meet the needs of a growing nation. The checks and balances system also gives both Congress and the president the ability to counteract each other.

Categorizing the Powers of Congress

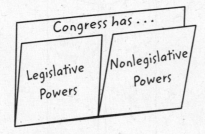

🖐 Two-Tab Book

The powers of Congress fall into two categories—legislative and non-legislative. Have students create a Two-Tab Foldable to keep notes about each type of power as they read the text.

Materials Needed: one sheet of 8.5" x 11" paper, scissors.

Sequencing Shifts in Power

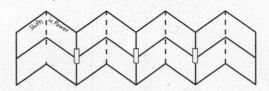

🖐 Accordion Book

Students can create an Accordion Book to help them visualize the competition for and shifts in power between Congress and the president. Have students add entries for relevant dates and events to their time lines as they read the text.

Materials Needed: two sheets of 8.5" x 11" paper, scissors, stapler or glue.

Outlining Additional Powers of Congress

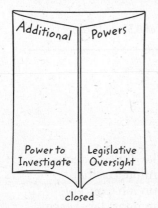

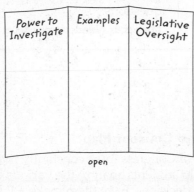

◖ Tri-Fold Book

Students can create a Tri-Fold Book to aid in their study of the additional powers of Congress. As they read the text, students should make notes that answer the questions: what, why, and how pertaining to congressional power to investigate and also legislative oversight. The center column should be used to note examples of each type of power.

Materials Needed: one sheet of 8.5" x 11" paper.

CHAPTER 7

Congress at Work

TOPIC SUMMARY

The primary task of Congress is to review proposed legislation and make decisions accordingly. Before it can receive presidential approval, a bill must pass through both houses of Congress. Members of Congress vote on thousands of issues, as well as assist their constituents directly as needed.

Identifying Types of Bills

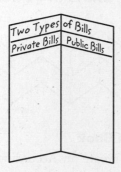

🔔 Two-Column Chart

Have students make a Two-Column Chart to identify facts about the two types of bills—private and public. On each side of the chart, students should note the definition of each type and other facts gathered from the text.

Materials Needed: one sheet of 8.5" x 11" paper.

Analyzing Taxing and Spending

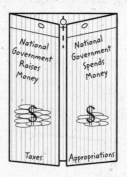

🔔 Shutter Fold

A Shutter Fold will give students a visual aid to understanding taxes and appropriations. On the inside left of the shutter, students should record questions about the taxation process that are answered in the reading. For example: What are taxes? Who makes the rules about taxes? On the inside right of the shutter, students should record questions about how money is appropriated. Students may then either answer the questions themselves, or exchange with a partner to answer questions.

Materials Needed: one sheet of 8.5" x 11" paper.

Analyzing Influences on Congress

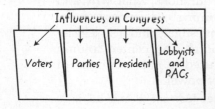

↩ Four-Tab Concept Map

Members of Congress must constantly make difficult decisions. To help students analyze the various influences that shape these decisions, have them make a Four-Tab Concept Map titled "Influences on Congress." Have students label each of the four tabs *Voters, Parties, President,* and *Lobbyists and PACs.* Inside each of the tabs, students should record the ways in which each group influences the decisions Congress makes.

Materials Needed: one sheet of 8.5" x 11" paper, scissors.

CHAPTER 8

The Presidency

TOPIC SUMMARY

The office of the president has been developing since the birth of our nation. During this time, the powers of the president have changed to match the needs of the changing country. The method of electing a president, however, has not changed. The Electoral College ultimately selects the president and vice president. Once elected, the president selects a cabinet to advise and help make decisions.

Summarizing the Presidency

🔵 Folded Chart

Have students prepare a Folded Chart to summarize five aspects of the presidency. Students should fold the paper into sixths to form rows, then fold in a hotdog fold to form two columns. As they read, students can fill in the right side of the chart with facts learned from the text about the duties, term, salary, qualifications, and succession of the president.

Materials Needed: one sheet of 8.5" x 11" paper.

Analyzing the Election Process

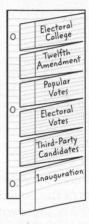

🔵 Six-Tab Book

Have students create a Six-Tab Foldable to analyze the process by which a president and vice president are elected. Each of the tabs should be labeled with one of the following: *Electoral College, Twelfth Amendment, Popular Votes, Electoral Votes, Third-Party Candidates,* and *Inauguration.* Under each of the tabs, students should define the term and note the role of each in the election process.

Materials Needed: one sheet of 8.5" x 11" paper, scissors.

Researching the Inner Cabinet

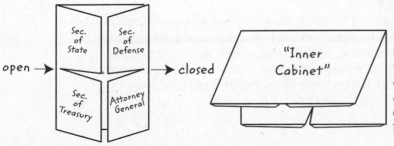

◖ Four-Door Book

Have students conduct research to learn more about the role and responsibilities of each of the four secretaries of the president's Inner Cabinet. The "doors" should be labeled *Secretary of State, Secretary of Defense, Secretary of Treasury,* and *Attorney General.* Inside each tab, students should record facts they gather in their research.

Materials Needed: one sheet of 11" x 17" paper, scissors.

CHAPTER 9

Presidential Leadership

TOPIC SUMMARY

The president of the United States in an extremely powerful person. Most of the powers and roles of the president are defined by the Constitution. Still others have evolved as the needs of a growing nation have changed. The most important leadership trait of a president is the strong ability to communicate.

Classifying Presidential Powers

Presidential Powers	
Constitutional Powers	
Informal Sources of Power	
Limits on Pres. Power	

☝ Folded Chart

Have students make a Folded Chart to classify the various powers of the president, and the limits on presidential power. Students should create a chart with three categories. Have students label the left side of the chart *Constitutional Powers, Informal Sources of Power,* and *Limits on Presidential Power.* Then, using information from the text, students should write a definition of each type of power, or list examples of each, in their appropriate categories.

Materials Needed: one sheet of 8.5" x 11" paper.

Explaining the Roles of the President

☝ Layered Book

The president has seven key duties. Have students create a Layered Book to explain each of the president's roles. Students should title their book, "Roles of the President." Then, students should label the tabs with one of the following: *Head of State, Chief Executive, Chief Legislator, Economic Planner, Party Leader, Chief Diplomat,* and *Commander in Chief.* Inside, students should explain the duties required and note whether this duty is mandated by the Constitution or has evolved over time.

Materials Needed: four sheets of 8.5" x 11" paper, stapler, or glue.

Researching Key Terms

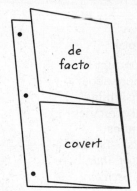

◖ Two-Tab Book

Have students create a Two-Tab Book for the key terms from this section. Students should conduct research to define and give examples, other than those in the text, of the terms *de facto* and *covert* as they relate to leadership in government. Students can find Internet encyclopedia articles to enrich their understanding of these concepts.

Materials Needed: one sheet of 8.5" x 11" paper, scissors.

CHAPTER 10

The Federal Bureaucracy

TOPIC SUMMARY

Hundreds of agencies make up the federal bureaucracy. They are organized as cabinet departments, independent agencies, and regulatory commissions. The majority of these departments and agencies belong to the executive branch and help to see that laws are carried out. The civil-service system ensures that people are able to keep their government jobs regardless of whether they personally support the administration in office or not.

Classifying Bureaucracies

Bureaucratic Organizations	Purposes	Examples
Independent Agencies		
Regulatory Commissions		

⬆ Folded Table

Many of the bureaucracies of the government fall into different classifications. Have students make a Folded Table to classify two types, *Independent Agencies* and *Regulatory Commissions*. Students can use information from the text to list the purposes and some examples of each.

Materials Needed: one sheet of 11" x 17" paper.

Comparing Federal Systems

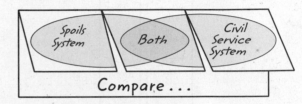

Compare . . .

⬆ Three-Tab Venn Diagram

To better understand the history of the civil-service system, have students make a Three-Tab Venn Diagram. On the left tab, have students explain the history and practices of the spoils system. On the right tab, have them do the same for the civil-service system. On the center tab, students should list the advantages and disadvantages of both systems.

Materials Needed: one sheet of 8.5" x 11" paper, scissors.

Defining Key Terms

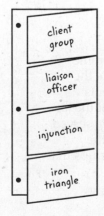

↩ Vocabulary Book

A Vocabulary Book will help students to better understand the intricacies of government bureaucracy. Have students create a Four-Tab Book. On each of the tabs, students should define the following terms: *client group, liaison officer, injunction,* and *iron triangle*. Students could also do further research to give examples of each of the four terms other than those found in the text.

Materials Needed: one sheet of 8.5" x 11" paper, scissors.

CHAPTER 11

The Federal Court System

TOPIC SUMMARY

The Supreme Court was created by the Constitution as a way of balancing the power between the other two branches of government. The lower federal courts, however, hear most of the cases. These courts are divided into either constitutional federal courts or legislative federal courts. Federal courts are able to hear cases involving federal laws, treaties, and interpretation of the Constitution. State courts have jurisdiction over cases involving state laws.

Explaining *Marbury v. Madison*

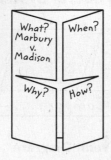

🔓 Four-Door Book

One of the most famous court cases in U.S. history is *Marbury* v. *Madison*. Have students prepare a Four-Door Foldable to better understand this landmark decision. Under each of the "doors," students should record information that thoroughly answers the questions *What, When, Why,* and *How.* Student may expand their information by conducting their own research.

Materials Needed: one sheet of 11" x 17" paper, scissors.

Comparing Federal Court Systems

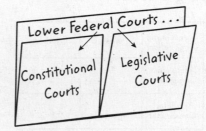

🔓 Two-Tab Concept Map

Have students create a Two-Tab Concept Map to compare and contrast two lower federal court systems—the *Constitutional Courts* and the *Legislative Courts.*

Materials Needed: one sheet of 8.5" x 11" paper, scissors.

Analyzing the Supreme Court

🔓 Layered Book

A Layered Book will help students analyze the Supreme Court. Under the first tab, students should summarize the jurisdiction of the Court. Under the second tab, students should explain the composition of the Court, duties of the justices, and the historical background of those who have served as justices. For the third tab, students should outline the process by which justices are appointed, including groups that influence the decision.

Materials Needed: two sheets of 8.5" x 11" paper, stapler or glue.

CHAPTER 12

Supreme Court Decision Making

TOPIC SUMMARY

The Supreme Court is the highest court in the land. Hearing cases from prisoners to presidents, the Supreme Court has the final ruling in all cases involving federal law. The justices choose the cases they hear based on the constitutional issues these cases raise. The Supreme Court is very powerful because when it makes a decision, it is determining public policy.

Charting Supreme Court Procedures

Tri-Fold Book

Have students prepare a Tri-Fold Book to chart the procedures of the Supreme Court. Students should fold their paper into thirds to make a three-column chart. In the first column, students can make a bulleted list of the procedures used by the Court during each sitting. In the second column, have students outline the two ways in which cases come to the Court. Finally, in the third column, students should outline the steps the Court takes in deciding major cases.

Materials Needed: one sheet of 8.5" x 11" paper.

Analyzing Limits on the Court

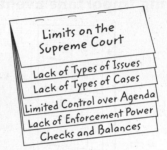

Layered Book

A Layered Book will help students analyze the limits to power of the Supreme Court. Students should create a Foldable with six tabs. They should title the first tab *Limits on the Supreme Court.* On the second tab they should note the limits on types of issues the Court can rule on. The third tab should be used to list the types of cases the Court cannot hear. The fourth tab should explain the Court's limited control over the agenda. On the fifth tab, students should give an overview of the Court's lack of enforcement power. Finally, on the sixth tab, students should explain the system of checks and balances on the Court.

Materials Needed: three sheets of 8.5" x 11" paper, glue or stapler.

Examining the Court's Power

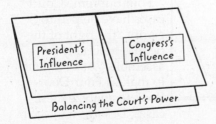

Two-Tab Book

Have students create a Two-Tab Foldable to examine the influences of the other two branches of government on the Supreme Court. On the left tab, students should record the ways in which the president influences the Court. On the right tab, students should list the ways in which the Court is influenced by Congress. This will give students a more complete understanding of the ways in which the three branches of government interact.

Materials Needed: one sheet of 8.5" x 11" paper, scissors.

CHAPTER 13

Constitutional Freedoms

TOPIC SUMMARY

The Constitution guarantees all citizens of the United States certain rights. The first ten amendments to the Constitution, the Bill of Rights, secure various freedoms for all U.S. citizens. Among these rights are freedom of religion, freedom of speech, and freedom of assembly. Over time, various cases have been brought before the courts to further interpret the extent of these freedoms.

Identifying Important Events

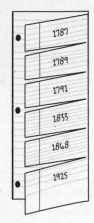

🏵 Six-Tab Book

Have students make a Six-Tab Book with the following dates: *1787, 1789, 1791, 1833, 1868,* and *1925.* Have students review the text to identify the importance of each date. On the inside of each tab, students should record the event that occurred in that year, and, if appropriate, explain its relevance to the development of the Bill of Rights.

Materials Needed: one sheet of 8.5" x 11" paper, scissors.

Comparing First Amendment Clauses

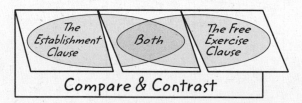

🏵 Three-Tab Venn Diagram

A Three-Tab Venn Diagram will help students compare and contrast the establishment clause and the free exercise clause of the First Amendment. On the left tab, students should write a brief definition of the establishment clause and list the ways it differs from the free exercise clause. On the right tab, students should do the same for the free exercise clause. On the center tab, students should list the ways both clauses protect freedom of religion.

Materials Needed: one sheet of 8.5" x 11" paper, scissors.

Analyzing Freedom of Assembly

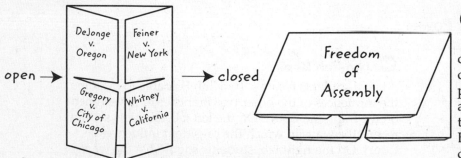

☝ Four-Door Book

Four Supreme Court cases have helped to clarify "the right of the people peaceably to assemble." Ask students to make a Four-Door Book to analyze these cases: *DeJonge* v. *Oregon, Feiner* v. *New York, Gregory* v. *City of Chicago,* and *Whitney* v. *California.* Under each of the "doors," students should briefly note the background of each of the cases and the issue it clarified.

Materials Needed: one sheet of 11" x 17" paper, scissors.

CHAPTER 14

Citizenship and Equal Justice

TOPIC SUMMARY

American citizens have many rights and responsibilities. Also living in our country are many aliens and immigrants who are not citizens. Naturalization is the process that grants immigrants U.S. citizenship if they wish. Everyone is entitled to equal rights and treatment under our law. Justice in a democracy means protecting the innocent from government police power as well as punishing the guilty.

Explaining Immigration Policy

Layered Book

Have students make a Layered Book to explain how immigration policy has changed over time. Students should review the text on each of the following subjects: *the Growth of Restrictions (1882–1924), National Origins Quotas (1924–1965), the Immigration Reform Act of 1965, the Immigration Reform and Control Act of 1986,* and *the Immigration Act of 1990.* After reviewing the text, students should record the main idea of each section on its appropriate tab of the Layered Book.

Materials Needed: three sheets of 8.5" x 11" paper, stapler or glue.

Classifying Equal Protection

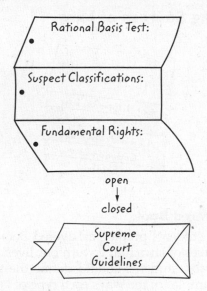

Tri-Fold Book

The Supreme Court has developed certain guidelines to test whether a state law or action violates citizens' rights to equal protection of the law. Have students create a Tri-Fold Book to further their understanding of how the Court applies each of the following tests: *the rational basis test, suspect classifications,* and *fundamental rights.* Have students define each of these tests and give examples of how they have been applied.

Materials Needed: one sheet of 8.5" x 11" paper.

Evaluating Civil Liberties

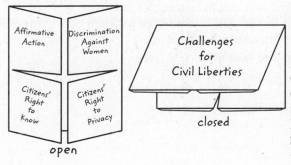

Four-Door Book

Students can create a Four-Door Book titled "Challenges for Civil Liberties" to gain a clearer understanding of how our laws often evolve to meet the needs of society. For each of the four "doors," students should make bulleted lists of the main points from the text. Students may finish each section by writing their personal opinion about whether each area needs more or less legislation.

Materials Needed: one sheet of 11" x 17" paper.

CHAPTER 15

Law in America

TOPIC SUMMARY

The hallmark of our democratic society is that decisions and actions are made according to established laws rather than by arbitrary actions and decrees. The overarching principles of the American justice system are equal justice under the law, due process of law, the adversary system of justice, and the presumption of innocence. Civil and criminal laws work to protect citizens and to resolve conflicts in everyday life.

Tracing Sources of Law

🔖 Layered Book

Have students prepare a Layered Book to trace the sources of laws that govern our lives. For each of the tabs, students should define the term and give examples of the ways each type of law affects daily life. The top tab should be labeled *Laws*. The remaining tabs should be labeled *Constitutional Law, Statutory Law, Administrative Law, Common Law,* and *Equity*.

Materials Needed: three sheets of 8.5"x 11" paper, stapler or glue.

Categorizing Civil Laws

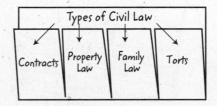

🔖 Four-Tab Book

Have students create a Four-Tab Foldable to categorize the four types of civil law: *contracts, property law, family law,* and *torts*. Under each tab, students should explain the terms and list examples of that type of law. Students may also conduct research into any ways these areas of law have changed over time.

Materials Needed: one sheet of 8.5" x 11" paper.

Classifying Crime

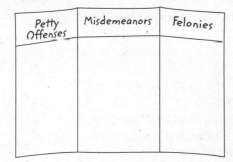

◖ Tri-Fold Chart

Crimes can be classified into three main categories: *petty offenses, misdemeanors,* and *felonies*. Have students review the text and list examples of each type of crime and the usual consequences for each type on the appropriate area of the chart.

Materials Needed: one sheet of 8.5" x 11" paper.

CHAPTER 16

Political Parties

TOPIC SUMMARY

A political party is a group of people with broad common interests who organize to win elections, control government, and thereby influence government policies. Around the world, various party systems exist, but the United States has a two-party system. Each party nominates candidates for office and works to have its candidates elected. However, even when a party loses an election, it has a role to play as a government "watchdog."

Evaluating Third Parties

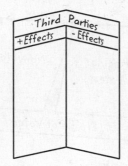

⬆ Two-Column Chart

After students have read about the role of third parties, have them make a Two-Column Chart. On the left side of the chart, students should list any of the positive effects that third parties have on the election process. On the right side of the chart, students should list the negative effects of third-party candidates in an election.

Materials Needed: one sheet of 8.5" x 11" paper.

Defining Key Terms

⬆ Vocabulary Book

Have students create an Eight-Tab Vocabulary Book to reinforce their understanding of the key terms from this section. Students should write a brief definition on the inside of the tab for each of the following terms: *independent, precinct, precinct captain, ward, state central committee, national convention, national committee,* and *patronage.*

Materials Needed: one sheet of 8.5" x 11" paper, scissors.

Describing Candidate Selection

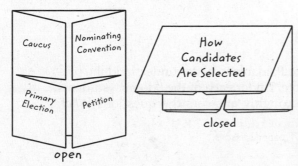

⬅ Four-Door Book

Candidates for office are usually selected in one of four ways: *caucus, nominating convention, primary election,* or *petition.* Have students make a Four-Door Book to describe each of these four ways an individual may be nominated. Students should briefly but completely describe each process.

Materials Needed: one sheet of 11" x 17" paper, scissors.

CHAPTER 17

Elections and Voting

TOPIC SUMMARY

A successful democracy is based on an informed electorate exercising their right to vote. Over time, the definition of who may vote in the United States has changed. Constitutional amendments have given African Americans, women, and citizens who are 18 years of age and older the right to vote. Still, many citizens choose not to exercise their right to choose elected officials.

Defining Key Terms

🖱 Vocabulary Book

Have students prepare a Four-Tab Vocabulary Book to enhance their understanding of the key terms associated with election campaigns. Students should use one of the four tabs to define each of the following terms: *campaign manager, image, political action committee,* and *soft money.* After they have defined the terms, have students also use each word in a sentence on the inside of the tab.

Materials Needed: one sheet of 8.5" x 11" paper, scissors.

Comparing Voters and Nonvoters

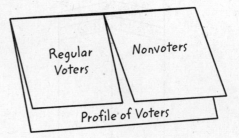

🖱 Two-Tab Book

Have students make a Two-Tab Book to compare characteristics of those citizens who vote regularly and those who do not. On the left tab, students should make a bulleted list of the factors most regular voters have in common. On the right tab, students should list the reasons given in the text to explain why many citizens do not vote.

Materials Needed: one sheet of 8.5" x 11" paper, scissors.

Describing Voter Registration

🖱 Four-Door Book

Have students prepare a Four-Door Foldable to better understand the procedures involved in registering to vote. Under each of the "doors," students should record information that thoroughly answers the questions *What, When, Where,* and *How.*

Materials Needed: one sheet of 11" x 17" paper, scissors.

CHAPTER 18

Interest Groups and Public Opinion

TOPIC SUMMARY

An interest group is a group of people who share common goals and organize to influence government. The role of the interest group is to help bridge the gap between citizens and the government. Interest groups may employ lobbyists or use financial contributions to political action committees to support the candidates that share their views. Public officials want to be responsive to citizens and use various means to gauge public opinion.

Identifying Interest Groups

⊙ Layered Book

A Layered Book will give students a handy reference guide to identifying various interest groups. Students should find examples in the text for each of the following categories of groups: *business and labor, agricultural,* and *other.* On the appropriate tab, students should make a bulleted list of the groups, and identify the populations they serve.

Materials Needed: two sheets of 8.5" x 11" paper, stapler or glue.

Comparing Influences to Public Policy

Compare	Purposes	Influences
Lobbyists		
PACs		

⊙ Folded Table

Have students prepare this Foldable to compare the contributions of lobbyists and PACs to public policy. After students have read the text, they should fill in each of the cells of the table. Under the heading *Purposes,* students should summarize the reason for the existence of each of the groups. Under the heading *Influences,* students should list the methods employed by each group to affect public policy.

Materials Needed: one sheet of 11" x 17" paper.

Exploring Public Opinion

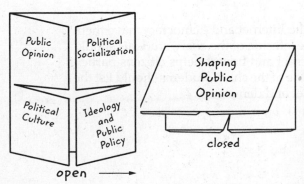

◖ Four-Door Book

Have students make a Four-Door Book to explore various aspects of how we think about the issues that shape our lives. Under the first door, students should explain the nature of public opinion. Under the second door, have students summarize the process of political socialization. The third door of this Foldable should be used to evaluate political culture. Finally, the fourth door should be used to review ideology and public policy.

Materials Needed: one sheet of 11" x 17" paper, scissors.

CHAPTER 19

The Mass Media

TOPIC SUMMARY

We depend on the mass media for news, entertainment, and information. Mass media influences individuals, interest groups, and government. Government, in turn, can also influence the media. The First Amendment guarantees freedom from censorship, but federal regulations try to balance this right against protecting citizens from harmful or offensive content.

Analyzing Media Impact on Government

🔲 Five-Tab Book

A Five-Tab Book will be useful for students to analyze the media's impact on government. Have students title the Foldable "The Media and . . ." and label each of the tabs as follows: *The President, Presidential Campaigns, The Congress, The Court,* and *The Public.* Under each tab, students should record the ways in which the media and each person or group have a mutually beneficial relationship.

Materials Needed: one sheet of 8.5" x 11" paper, scissors.

Evaluating Regulation of the Media

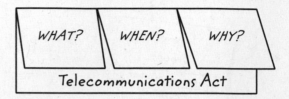

🔲 Three-Tab Book

Have students make a Three-Tab Foldable to fully evaluate the Telecommunications Act of 1996. Under the first tab, students should briefly explain the five issues covered by the act. Under the second tab, students should write when the act was passed by Congress. Under the third tab, have students explain why Congress felt the act was necessary.

Materials Needed: one sheet of 8.5" x 11" paper, scissors.

Summarizing the Role of the Internet

◖ Two-Column Chart

After students have read about the Internet and democracy, have them make a Two Column Chart. On the left side of the chart, students should list the various benefits of the Internet and how it helps citizens participate in a democracy. On the right side of the chart, students should list the challenges pertaining to the Internet and democracy.

Materials Needed: one sheet of 8.5" x 11" paper.

CHAPTER 20

Taxing and Spending

TOPIC SUMMARY

The services provided by the government cost money. Government must therefore raise revenue to pay for services through taxes and loans. The government must provide an annual budget to account for how revenue will be spent. Budget decisions influence the economy by encouraging or discouraging spending and saving by citizens.

Comparing Revenue Sources

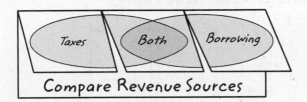

Three-Tab Venn Diagram

Have students make a Three-Tab Venn Diagram to compare the government's sources of revenue. On the left tab, students should list the various types of taxes government collects. On the right tab, students should list the instruments that government uses to borrow money. On the center tab, students should compare the advantages and disadvantages of both sources of raising revenue.

Materials Needed: one sheet of 8.5" x 11" paper, scissors.

Federal Budget

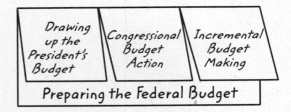

Three-Tab Book

Students may gain a better understanding of the preparation of the federal budget by making this Foldable. On the left tab, students should summarize the process of drawing up the president's budget. On the center tab, they will review congressional budget action. Finally, on the third tab, students can briefly explain incremental budget making.

Materials Needed: one sheet of 8.5" x 11" paper, scissors.

Tracing Spending

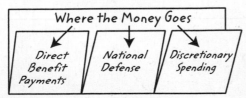

Three-Tab Concept Map

Where does all the money the government collects go? Students can answer this question with a Three-Tab Concept Map. Students should create a tab for each of the following: *Direct Benefit Payments*, *National Defense*, and *Discretionary Spending*. Under each tab, students should define each category and trace the amount of money allocated for each area.

Materials Needed: one 8.5" x 11" sheet of paper, scissors.

CHAPTER 21

Social and Domestic Policy

TOPIC SUMMARY

National policy affects your economic decisions, your education, your health, and much more. Although free enterprise is the foundation of the American economic system, ours is a mixed economy. In addition to promoting and regulating business, the federal government also protects and regulates labor unions, agriculture, the environment, health care, public assistance, education, housing, and transportation.

Relating Policy

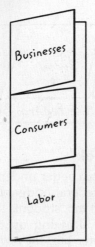

🎧 Three-Tab Book

With this Foldable, students can create a guide to understanding the government policies affecting private enterprise. Have students review the text and make notes under each tab about the way government both supports and regulates business, consumers, and labor.

Materials Needed: one sheet of 8.5" x 11" paper, scissors.

Summarizing Agriculture and Environment Policy

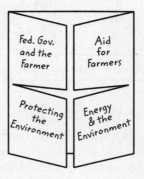

🎧 Four-Door Book

Have students make a Four-Door Book. The four "doors" should be labeled as follows: *Federal Government and the Farmer, Aid for Farmers, Protecting the Environment,* and *Energy and the Environment.* Under each door, students should summarize the major points found in the text for each subject.

Materials Needed: one sheet of 11" x 17" paper, scissors.

Outlining Education, Housing, and Transportation

Education	Housing	Transportation

🌀 Folded Chart

Have students create a Folded Chart to outline what they have learned about the federal government's role in each of the following: *Education, Housing,* and *Transportation.* In each column student should outline the major points from the text. As a last point for each category, students may add their own opinions about what more the government should do for each area.

Materials Needed: one sheet of 11" x 17" paper.

CHAPTER 22

Foreign Policy and Defense

TOPIC SUMMARY

The United States today confronts global challenges. However, the primary goal of American foreign policy is to preserve national security. The executive and legislative branches share foreign policy powers. The Department of State promotes the long-range security and well-being of the United States, while the Department of Defense defends the nation. The U.S. government uses diplomatic tools such as alliances, foreign aid, and economic sanctions in foreign relations. When diplomacy fails, however, military action is sometimes necessary.

Defining Key Terms

🔊 Vocabulary Book

Ask students to create a Five-Tab Vocabulary Book with the following terms: *foreign policy, national security, isolationism, internationalism,* and *containment.* Under each tab, students should define the term. To extend the activity, students could use the back of the Foldable to write an imaginary newspaper article using each of the key terms.

Materials Needed: one sheet of 8.5" x 11" paper, scissors.

Comparing Powers

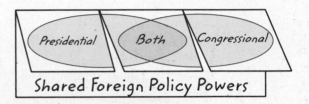

🔊 Three-Tab Venn Diagram

A Venn Diagram Foldable will give students a tool for comparing the foreign policy powers of the president and Congress. On the left tab, students should summarize the powers of the president. On the right tab, students should detail the powers of Congress. On the center tab, students can explain how the president and Congress work together in the foreign-policy arena.

Materials Needed: one sheet of 8.5" x 11" paper, scissors.

Analyzing Policy in Action

⟲ Layered Book

Have students make a Layered Book to analyze the tools of foreign policy. The top tab should be labeled "Foreign Policy in Action." On the remaining three tabs students should write: *Alliances and Pacts, Foreign Aid Programs,* and *Sanctions and Force.* Then, students can summarize the most important points from the text on the inside of the appropriate tab.

Materials Needed: two sheets of 8.5" x 11" paper, glue or stapler.

CHAPTER 23

Structure and Function of State Government

TOPIC SUMMARY

State government touches your life every day. Like the federal Constitution, state constitutions provide for three branches of government and protection of individual rights. The major areas of concern for most states include the regulation of business, the administration and control of natural resources, the protection of individual rights, and welfare programs. Nearly half the general revenue of state governments comes from state taxes. Other sources of revenue are borrowing, lotteries, license fees, and the federal government.

Summarizing State Government

🔴 Layered Book

A Layered Book will give students a tool to help summarize the branches of state government. State governments, like the federal government, are divided into legislative, executive, and judicial branches. For each of the tabs, students should answer the questions: *Who are the members of this branch?*; *How are they put into office?*; and *What is their primary function?*

Materials Needed: two sheets of 8.5" x 11" paper, stapler, or glue.

Classifying State Government Policy

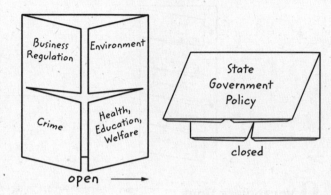

🔴 Four-Door Book

Students can explore state government's four major policy areas with this Foldable. The four "doors" should be labeled: *Business Regulation, Environment, Crime,* and *Health, Education, Welfare.* For each category, students should give a summary of how state government addresses the problem of each area.

Materials Needed: one sheet of 11" x 17" paper, scissors.

Explaining State Taxes

Sales Tax	
State Income Tax	
Other Taxes	

🔵 Tri-Fold Chart

Have students create a Tri-Fold Chart to explain the taxes that state governments collect. The chart should have three categories: *Sales Tax, State Income Tax,* and *Other Taxes.* After students have read the text, have them explain the various taxes in the appropriate place on the chart.

Materials Needed: one sheet of 8.5" x 11" paper.

CHAPTER 24

Structure and Function of Local Government

TOPIC SUMMARY

Local government is the form of government closest and most accessible to you. Local governments provide citizens with basic services such as education, police and fire protection, water, and sewage and sanitation. Some forms of local government include counties, townships, municipalities, and special districts. Local government is usually financed with property taxes. Some challenges faced by local government include housing shortages, inadequate transportation, pollution, poverty, and crime.

Describing Local Government

🖐 Layered Book

There are several types of local governments. Have students make a Layered Book to describe the following five types: *county, township, New England Town, municipality,* and *special district.* Students should create bulleted list on the inside of each tab of important points from the text.

Materials Needed: three sheets of 8.5" x 11" paper, stapler or glue.

Defining Key Terms

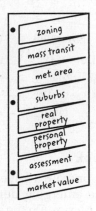

🖐 Vocabulary Book

Have students make a Vocabulary Book to reinforce their understanding of the key terms. Students should make a tab for each of the following terms: *zoning, mass transit, metropolitan area, suburbs, real property, personal property, assessment,* and *market value.* Students should then define each term on the inside of the tab.

Materials Needed: one sheet of 8.5" x 11" paper, scissors.

Reporting on Urban Growth

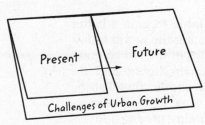

🖐 Two-Tab Book

What are the challenges of urban growth? Have students create a Two-Tab Book to report on their understanding of the challenges we face today, as well as those we will most likely face in the future. Students should especially note how those problems are being or can be addressed.

Materials Needed: one sheet of 8.5" x 11" paper, scissors.

CHAPTER 25

Political Systems in Today's World

TOPIC SUMMARY

Various forms of political systems are in effect around the world. Some countries are consolidated democracies, such as Great Britain, France, and Japan. They have free elections, constitutional government, and competing political parties. Some countries, such as Poland, South Africa, and Mexico, are emerging democracies. Many countries, however, are authoritarian states like Cuba and the People's Republic of China. They are headed by religious or military leaders. Organizations like NATO and the UN contribute to global security.

Examining Emerging Democracies

🕮 Layered Book

Have students prepare a Layered Book to better understand three emerging democracies: *Poland, South Africa,* and *Mexico.* On the appropriate tab for each, students should note the history of the movement toward democracy and the struggles each country has faced.

Materials Needed: two sheets of 8.5" x 11" paper, stapler or glue.

Analyzing Authoritarian States

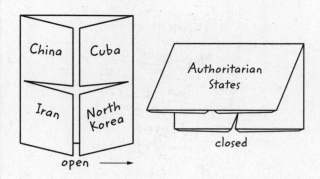

🕮 Four-Door Book

Many governments around the world are authoritarian states. Students can analyze four such states with this Foldable. Have students prepare a "door" for each of the following countries: *China, Cuba, Iran,* and *North Korea.* Students should then use information from the text to record the major points about each country.

Materials Needed: one sheet of 11" x 17" paper, scissors.

Evaluating Global Issues

	Issues	Solutions
Terrorism		
Nuclear Proliferation		
Human Rights		
The Environment		

☛ Folded Table

Have students prepare a Folded Table to gain a better understanding of the global issues facing the world today. Have students list the following topics in the left column: *Terrorism, Nuclear Proliferation, Human Rights,* and *the Environment.* For each topic, students should then list the issues or concerns surrounding the topic as well as solutions that have been proposed or implemented to address the concerns.

Materials Needed: one sheet of 11" x 17" paper.

CHAPTER 26

Development of Economic Systems

TOPIC SUMMARY

Today's world is truly a global economy. The world's people live in a variety of economic systems, including capitalism, socialism, and communism. Capitalism is characterized by private ownership of industry and services, individual initiative, competition, freedom of choice, and profit or loss. Mixed economies share the same factors and characteristics as pure capitalism, but they also integrate government regulation. Some developing nations have adopted forms of communism and socialism.

Comparing Emerging Economies

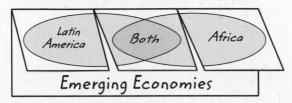

❶ Three-Tab Venn Diagram

This Foldable will give students a tool to help them understand the emerging economies of Latin America and Africa. On the left tab, students should summarize the challenges Latin America faces. They should do the same for Africa on the right tab. On the center tab, students should note the problems common to the economies of both regions.

Materials Needed: one sheet of 8.5" x 11" paper, scissors.

Sequencing Economies in Transition

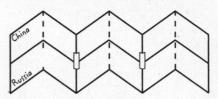

❶ Time Line

Many nations around the world are working to develop market economies. Have students create a time line to chronicle significant dates and events in the economic transitions of Russia and China. Students should list entries for China in the top half of the time line and entries for Russia in the bottom half. Students may also conduct research to add information about the current state of affairs in each country.

Materials Needed: one sheet of of 8.5" x 11" paper, stapler or glue.

Analyzing Trade

◗ Three-Tab Book

Have students prepare a Three-Tab Book to analyze three trade agreements covered in the text. Students should make a tab for each of the following: *WTO*, *EU*, and *NAFTA*. Under each tab, students should explain the history, purpose, and goals of each agreement listed.

Materials Needed: one sheet of 8.5" x 11" paper.